The Underdog Advantage

REWRITE YOUR FUTURE BY
TURNING YOUR DISADVANTAGES
INTO YOUR SUPERPOWERS

DEAN GRAZIOSI

ISBN   978-0-578-56846-1 *Hardcover*
       978-1-7334981-0-4 *Audiobook*
       978-1-7334981-1-1 *Ebook*

To everyone who ever felt like they were dealt a tough hand, thought of giving up, considered settling for an "ok" life—but still keeps pushing forward even when others and that inner voice say "enough." Your next level lives on the other side of one of those obstacles. So keep climbing.

And to my wife Lisa, and my children, Breana and Brody, thank you for loving me the way you do. You inspire me to be a better man every day. My love for you has transcended anything I could have ever imagined. If all else were gone, I'd still be the wealthiest man alive because of you.

Contents

The Underdog Advantage

I should be drinking tea, eating crumpets, driving on the wrong side of the road, and bowing to the Queen.

You know why I'm not?

Because of an underdog.

One single person, a man who was an underdog his whole life, leading a group of men who were underestimated and dismissed, found a way to win a war against the biggest, baddest military machine the world had ever known.

You know who I'm talking about: George Washington, the father of America, of course.

I thought I knew the story. I mean, we learn it in elementary school, right? George Washington chopped down a cherry tree and told the truth about it, then he beat the British, formed a new nation, and became President. That's about what I remembered from school (I wasn't a very good student if you can't tell).

But I didn't realize how amazing the *actual* story of George Washington was. And when I read about it, it hit me that this is the story of every struggling underdog—like I have been most of my life, and you probably are too. In fact, if you see yourself as an underdog, I think the story of George Washington and the founding of America is maybe the most important story you will ever hear.

You know why? It's because of how he won.

He won because he was an underdog.

How could that be? How could being an underdog lead to victory? Don't you want to be the favorite, the one destined for greatness? The one with all the advantages and all the people behind you?

Well...what if I told you that being an underdog could actually be one of the greatest unfair advantages of your life?

You see, underdogs have certain traits they can turn into superpowers when used correctly. And in fact, when viewed properly, I think being an underdog is the best advantage you can have in life, and has been *the key to all the success I've had in my life.*

But before I tell you why being an underdog could actually be the rocket fuel for your next-level-of-life launch, I'm going to tell you the part of George Washington's story you probably don't know...

THE UNDERDOG'S HISTORY OF THE REVOLUTIONARY WAR

George Washington was born in America to a well-off family. But that's pretty much where his advantages stopped.

He was the fourth son of his father, so by the time he was old enough for school, there was no money left to send him. He had to learn everything on his own, at home, without a teacher. That seems pretty bad, right?

Actually he turned it into an advantage. Not going to school allowed him to focus exclusively on the subjects he liked, and he self-taught and mastered fields like math, surveying, draftsmanship, and map-making. This led to him becoming the youngest surveyor in Virginia and allowed him to find and buy the best frontier lands before others even knew they existed.

He learned early on how to use one of the main underdog

advantages: turning what most people would consider the anchor holding him back into the wind behind his sail. Changing the disadvantage into an advantage.

He was eventually made a Major in the Virginia Regiment (which was a colonial army that the British organized and supplied). His British superior officers didn't give him the same level of respect as they did the British-born enlisted men. They paid him far less money and gave him the left-over supplies. He could feel them making fun of him behind his back and he wasn't paranoid, they truly looked down on him. Did this bother him? Heck yes. But he didn't let it bring him down, in fact, he used it as fire to drive him more. Once again—he used a disadvantage to his advantage and let the bad treatment motivate him and his troops on a level most people could never comprehend.

What resulted from this disrespectful treatment was growing success, even though he got the toughest and worst missions, the ones no one else wanted. In one battle, even though he literally was sick with dysentery, he organized a rearguard action that allowed another general's army to escape and avoid being captured. He had two horses shot out from under him and had bullet holes in his hat and coat. His heroism and leadership gained acclaim throughout the colonies and Europe.

He turned their disrespect for him into motivation for himself and his men, which resulted in respect from people all over the world. Talk about using his underdog advantages!

It gets better, way better. Washington used the land he bought (plus his marriage to a wealthy widow) to become a successful planter. He was elected as a burgess, meaning he was a part of the representatives of the Colonies underneath the King of England. Here again, he was always looked down upon because he wasn't British born. And of course, England totally disrespected America by taxing them with no representation, and ignoring all the demands of the colonies.

I won't go over Paul Revere's ride, and the Declaration of Independence, and the start of the war, and all that. You probably know that, because that's the cool stuff taught in most classrooms. What I want to focus on here are two events that defined George Washington and showed how much of an underdog he was—and how he used it to win.

The war starts. The Americans kick the British out of Boston in the Boston Tea Party, and now the British are pissed. The King of England doesn't want to play games anymore, he wants to come and show the uppity colonists who's boss. They decide to come for New York City. Washington assembles about 7,500 troops to fortify it.

Now you gotta understand, those 7,500 men, most of them

didn't have shoes. They didn't have uniforms. They didn't have enough gun powder. They weren't trained. They were anywhere from fifteen to sixty years old. Basically a bunch of farmers with guns and knives. Some even had spears and bows and arrows!

England sends 30,000 soldiers; 10,000 of those are hired guns. They're Hessians from Germany, which are not only amazing fighters, they're pretty much ruthless. Like, they are the type that would rather bayonet you in the face than capture you, just for fun.

So you have the most ragtag bunch of soldiers that existed on the planet at that time, and they're going up against the greatest military force in the world. Trained and battle-hardened, with guns and ammunition and master strategists, and experienced generals.

So what happens? Do the underdogs win?

NO!

They get their asses kicked!

The British beat the Americans at every level. They lost New York. They lost Brooklyn. Then they lost Long Island. Then they lost Fort Washington. And then they lost Fort Lee in New Jersey. They couldn't even hold New Jersey!

Washington barely escapes with like, 5,500 troops of the original 7,500. They're pushed out, now they're running across New Jersey. Tired, beaten, no shelter, shoes on only 50 percent of them, minimal ammunition, and worst of all they are out of food. They're retreating in the snow and there's blood trails from people with no socks on. They're literally sleeping under leaves.

As you would imagine, a lot of soldiers start deserting. The British government at that time would give people pardons. If you bail out of the Revolutionary Army, they give you a pardon and some money. So people were running nonstop, and his army dwindles more.

At this time, everybody's starting to criticize Washington. Congress is starting to question all his decisions. His top generals are like, "George Washington doesn't know what he's doing."

So think about all that piled up, one thing on top of another. Congress isn't feeling it, people are deserting the army, every obstacle possible piled up against them and the strongest army in the world ready to hunt them down and finish them off. And even worse, people are turning against them in each little city, giving information back to the British army on where they are and where they're going.

I mean, I didn't learn any of this in school. I couldn't believe how bad it got for him, and I honestly couldn't see any way out for Washington and his army. When I read about this, I thought to myself, "Zero chance that he can win this." I know how the story ends, and I live in a Free AMERICA and I still thought this!!

But Washington had something that the British didn't have. They had always been the privileged, the British were the biggest empire the world had ever seen. They had been the opposite of an underdog for as long as anyone alive could remember.

But Washington had been told he was nothing his whole life by the British. He was passed over for promotion by the British Army because he wasn't a "professional" general. He didn't have the pedigree of being born in England. He didn't have the king's support. He only had half of America's support. His own mother was ruthless to him. He didn't have the money. He didn't have any of it. Nothing. The ULTIMATE UNDERDOG.

What no one could see from the outside was that he had a burning inner desire to prove something to himself and those that doubted him. He was tired of being told he wasn't good enough, he wasn't from the right family, he didn't have the right accent, he wasn't from the right schools. He was tired of being passed over by people he was better than. He wanted the freedom to be who he was, and he used that as motivation, for himself and his men. He felt like everyone was against him, and he found a way to turn his underdog disadvantages into his underdog advantages. Since he didn't have unlimited resources, he found a way to be resourceful. He found a way to be innovative.

He used this feeling as motivation to find a way forward. And the British never saw him coming.

Washington decides to do what they would least expect: attack on Christmas morning.

And not only that, the only way this is possible is for him to take his entire army across the Delaware River.

You have to understand, this was nuts. It was one of the worst winters ever. There were icebergs on the river!! No one wanted to be outside. The British assumed that Washington would stay on his side of the river and wait until it was warm to resume fighting, because that's what they were going to do. And beyond that, the closest army to him was the Hessians, who already whipped his rag-tag group of farmers in New York City.

The Hessians thought they would never have the nerve to cross a frozen river on Christmas with thousands of men, so they partied all night. They drank and they were festive and lazy with their guards.

So what does he do?

He knows he has to go for it. And he writes down on a piece of paper, before he plans this attack, where he's outnumbered, outgunned, and outmanned, he writes "Victory or Death."

And on Christmas Eve at midnight, he starts crossing the frozen Delaware River. And he's got thousands of men that need to cross before morning. Cannons, horses. It's snowing. It's raining. The wind is blowing. Everything seems to be working against him.

But he's not going to stop. He's got that power in him. The power that comes from resisting all those people telling him he can't do it. He's a joke, he's just some bumpkin farmer. He'll never beat the British.

He eventually crosses his army. Everyone gets across by 4:00 in the morning and they march on the Hessians. They take them completely by surprise and capture most of them, along with their supplies, in less than an hour.

After that first victory George Washington has against the British Empire on Christmas Day, he crosses another time and sneak-attacks the British again at Princeton on January 3, where they kill a British general and force a larger army to retreat.

They had defeated the world's best army twice in a week!!

That was the shift of the American Revolution. We all know what happens from there.

WHAT IS BEING AN UNDERDOG ACTUALLY LIKE?

Have you ever felt like an underdog?

When I say Underdog, I don't mean your life has to be tragic and you're living on the streets. It just feels like a few (or many) cards are stacked against you and if you could just get them out of the way, you could soar. You could unleash that next-level version of you to the world, only if...

But what if you were actually given gifts, wrapped inside what you think is a disadvantage? What if once you knew how to unlock it, you could have a superpower like Washington and so many others?

What if by the end of this book you were actually grateful for all the shit that's happened or currently happening in your life, because it was designed perfectly for your future greatness?

My writing style is simple and to the point. I write as I talk, and together we are going to fuel your next level of income, growth, happiness, confidence, and abundance by using the gifts you already have. We just need to help you unwrap them. Then give you the implementation process to make your next level real.

So let me ask you this. Have you ever felt like no one had faith in you? That no one backed you or supported you?

Maybe you feel stuck in your life? It doesn't look bad from the outside but you feel like a prisoner trapped in mediocrity.

Ever felt like others look down on you or think your goals are pipe dreams?

Maybe you made some bad decisions. Maybe you didn't really understand what you were up against.

You ever feel like you missed your chance? That no matter what you do, nothing ever moves you forward and you're spinning your wheels?

You ever feel like so many things in your life are a disadvantage? That no matter what happens, it always somehow ends up not working out in your favor?

Maybe you feel like the world is not designed for you—that it's made for the privileged, the winners, the ones who already possess all the advantages.

Well...what about George Washington?

Even though he is so respected now, George Washington started out as the quintessential underdog.

It's easy to look back on that now and dismiss this. I mean, George Washington is the Father of America, what's that got to do with you?

The fact is, he was a huge underdog. He was facing terrible odds.

But all he did was figure out how to use the advantages of being an underdog to propel himself forward and actually win.

If you are still skeptical, I get it. I came from where you came from.

I grew up in a small town of about 6,000 people in upstate New York. It seemed like everyone had something going for them but me, and it sucked.

This is who I was growing up:

I was short.

I had goofy teeth.

I was 4′ 9″ and ninety pounds going into tenth grade and the only one in my class who hadn't reached puberty yet. That was a lot of fun.

My parents had no money, no social standing, nothing. Just hardworking people trying to survive.

My parents got divorced when I was three. Lived with my Grandmother a lot, then at my Mom and new Stepdad's, and then moved in with my Dad when I was twelve. When I moved in with him, we lived in the bathroom of his house for the first six months or so since it was small enough to heat with an electric heater. There was no heat in the rest of the house yet.

I had a learning disability. I could barely read at all until sixth grade, and was in various special ed classes all the way through high school. And I have fond memories of Miss Thompson calling me stupid on a regular basis as she would say through her clenched teeth, "Just sound it out."

I never went to college. I couldn't even get into college.

I got divorced.

I finally started to gain momentum and lost all my money three different times because of plain old stupid decisions and being naive.

I've got way more stories about how messed up my life has been at various times—don't worry, you will read them all in hilarious and gory detail throughout the book.

Yet here I am...I'm married to the woman of my dreams, I live in the house of my dreams, I am a dedicated father to two amazing kids, and I get to spend my days helping other people realize their dreams.

How did I go from being such an underdog to that life?

I did the same basic thing that George Washington did:

I utilized the Underdog Advantages; I flipped my disadvantages into advantages, and used them to prove everyone wrong, not be left behind, and to squeeze out all the juice life has to offer.

WHAT IS AN UNDERDOG ADVANTAGE?

What if the outside world, and even your inner-self voice of doubt, has been lying to you since day one?

What if everything you thought was a disadvantage, was actually an advantage?

What if the things you thought were holding you back were actually superpowers—if only you saw them that way?

What if you were actually in a great position, and one or two small shifts could unlock the animal inside of you?

What if, by flipping the success switch to "On," by changing the framework on how you see things, you could unlock limitless potential, income, and abundance?

I know, I know, this sounds like a sales pitch. But this is exactly how I turned my life around, and I am so passionate about this stuff. I discovered all of this by accident, and once I got it, I made it my life's mission to teach it to others.

Ultimately, I believe that the idea behind the American Dream is the underdog story, where anyone, no matter how poor or weak or disadvantaged or where they live, can use what they do have to achieve victory. That's what this book is about:

I want to teach you about the Underdog Advantage, and how to use it in your life.

There are many different parts of the Underdog Advantage. Here is a list of what I will teach in this book. Many of them are similar, and some may or may not apply to you. I'm not saying this list is exhaustive either, in fact, you can probably think of more if you really tried.

What I did was think of all the Underdog Advantages I could, and then I organized them into chapters around the biggest ones, the ones that I see moving the needle toward success the most in my life and the lives of other people.

CHAPTER 1: UNDERDOGS HAVE NOTHING TO LOSE

The privileged are expected to win, but underdogs have nothing to lose and can compete without fear of loss. Underdogs have no one to impress, no expectations to meet, and nowhere to go but up, which takes all the pressure off of them.

CHAPTER 2: UNDERDOGS CAN USE "THE POWER OF YOU CAN'T"

The privileged may have already reached their goals and can struggle with remaining motivated, but underdogs can find motivation everywhere, and use it to their advantage. Underdogs have desperation and heartbreak that they can use as fuel to create action. And of course, Underdogs can use the "Power of You Can't" motivation. There is a reason they say in sports, it's the "Nobody believes in us" phrase that empowers victory over all else.

CHAPTER 3: UNDERDOGS ACT FAST AND IMPROVE QUICKLY

The privileged have to plan their actions carefully, but underdogs can take action immediately, and get momentum. Underdogs can also do more of what works and less of what doesn't, can focus on progress over perfection, and don't need to worry about getting everything right. Underdogs can easily get momentum, and then use it to rocket past people.

CHAPTER 4: UNDERDOGS ARE RELENTLESSLY RESOURCEFUL

The privileged are always being watched and have to follow the rules, but underdogs can operate on the margins, outside of view, without having to get permission. They can take more risks and go after bigger problems, with the knowledge that they aren't big or important enough to be stopped or restricted.

CHAPTER 5: UNDERDOGS CAN SELF-EDUCATE

The privileged have to pretend they know everything, but underdogs can admit they don't know things. This allows Underdogs to go get the help they need, use alternative learning strategies and take uncommon action to achieve their goals.

CHAPTER 6: UNDERDOGS DON'T HAVE TO CARE WHAT OTHER PEOPLE THINK

The privileged have to make everyone happy, but underdogs don't have to be concerned with what others think. They can grow in peace because no one is watching them and they are free to fail without much consequence. Underdogs can work on themselves without distraction, and because they are out of the spotlight, can see who their real friends are. Underdogs can find and utilize new ideas as well, without worrying about looking weird.

CHAPTER 7: UNDERDOGS CAN TURN DESPERATION INTO PERSUASION

The privileged don't need to be especially motivated, because they already have their status and their position. They aren't as hungry or desperate anymore. This might seem like an advantage, but it's not—because desperation is the very best fuel for persuasion. And without persuasion, nothing happens.

WHAT THIS BOOK IS NOT

Before we jump in, I want to be clear about what this book is not. It is NOT:

- A way to easily make money without doing any work

- A quick fix

- A few tips and tricks

- Something to read once and forget about

I'm sure you know that, but sometimes people get a little excited and expect things that are unrealistic. I like to manage expectations and to make sure going in that you really know what this is and what you can get.

To be clear, *The Underdog Advantage* is an entirely new way to look at your life, especially if you feel like an underdog and have not yet achieved what you desire out of life.

I'm not going to help you recreate yourself or become someone new. I believe you already have this power in you. All I want to do is help you see it, unlock it, embrace it, and then give you the tools to get your rocket ship off the ground.

I've been an underdog my whole life. Even now, when I have so much going for me, I still feel like an underdog.

In fact, I make sure to KEEP the underdog mindset.

Why would I keep that mindset, when I am so clearly and objectively NOT an underdog anymore?

Because that mindset is such a big advantage.

Underdogs have to be innovative. They have to be creative, because they don't have all the assets somebody else has.

Underdogs have a passion to prove themselves.

Underdogs are people that you never see coming.

Underdogs are always underestimated.

Underdogs can harness the power that comes from people telling them they can't.

What if being an underdog was your gift. What if it was actually meant to be your journey. It was there to provide you the difficulties you needed to sharpen your tools and become the person you needed to become. What if your problems were actually the catapult to put you above the rest?

History is a great teacher of what's possible. Think about George Washington, or read any history book, look back at the people that have changed the world, have changed the legacy for their families—because they didn't give in.

At some point in all of our lives we've all felt like no one was in our corner. That it was too hard to start the business. That people have already done what you want to do. That it's the wrong timing. It's the wrong government. You come from the wrong pedigree. Your parents don't support you. Your husband, your wife stands in your way.

You have an underdog story. I have my own. We all feel like we're an underdog in some way, shape, or form.

We can use that as our anchor and say, "Poor me. I wasn't born with the right things. No one supports me. I don't have the money." Whether that's from your family, your financial situation, where you live, what you do for a living, your education, your supposed capabilities, knowledge, and expertise, we all feel it.

I know you've felt that way. I know because I've felt that way. Hell, I STILL feel that way at times.

Let me warn you: you might get offended by some of the ways I challenge you in this book.

And I don't doubt that many of you might be going through some tough times as you read this.

But when I think about people like George Washington and read stories like the ones that are coming—about famous people you know, and average people just like you, who have used these techniques—when I read the stories in which they had so much worse things against them, it motivates me. They had so many obstacles in front of them.

But they turned their disadvantages into advantages. They made an impact. And when they had the big machine against them, they won.

And I want you to win.

This book is the way.

Let's get started.

CHAPTER 1

Underdogs Have Nothing to Lose

I was full-on crying—I'm talking about heaving, ugly, sobbing, hyperventilating crying—I was twenty-six years old and I thought I'd peaked.

I was sitting on the floor Indian style, rocking back and forth, looking out the window of my hotel room down onto the Sunset Strip in Hollywood, California.

Only two hours earlier, I'd agreed in principle to a deal with two of the biggest stars in the world to help them create a ground-breaking new website, back in the early days of the internet (1994). I'd come from nowhere, with no chance to get it, and I got the deal. It was the ultimate underdog triumph.

I left the meeting and drove around Sunset Boulevard in

a rented convertible, the sun on my face, and I was feeling so fulfilled and totally high on life. I'd arrived. I was in Hollywood, and I found a next-level piece of significance that I craved.

So why was I crying like a six-year-old who had lost their favorite blanket or stuffed animal?

I lost the deal, and with it, the importance and the significance I'd gotten from it. I thought this was going to be the catapult to get me out of my little town, to be something bigger, and just like that it was gone. I reached for that brass ring, and I thought I had it…only to have it ripped away from me.

Here's the thing with this story: I didn't eventually get the deal. I never found a way to make it work. I just failed, and I cried, and that's it. Or was it?

You see: I didn't actually lose anything. In fact, looking back at that failure (or tragedy as I perceived it), I now see it was actually designed specifically for me. Maybe a test to see if I was worthy of a next-level life, or to build my success muscle.

And learning that changed my whole life.

THE PRIVILEGED ARE EXPECTED TO WIN

Everyone looks at those with the cards stacked in their favor and expects them to win. If anything it's a letdown if they *don't* win. That's what makes them privileged after all—they're the ones who are supposed to win all the time. They are the favorites.

But underdogs, no one expects anything from them. If they lose, so what? They were supposed to lose. They didn't have a shot anyway.

When you look at this from the outside, it's kind of depressing. That tall, handsome, tan, good-looking, rich guy, who wins everything—why does he need more? Why does he need to win again? Can't he take a few rounds off, give me a chance?

I mean, it seems like he has all the advantages, right? And once someone has a lead like that, where do they go? It seems like they never lose. It seems like they keep winning forever.

Wouldn't that be great, to be the big shot, to be expected to win, and just cruise to victory every time?

But lemme ask you: is that how it really works? Do the privileged actually just cruise to victory?

Yeah, I guess, sometimes.

But here's the thing you aren't seeing: that the one with the "so-called" advantages *has to win*. All the pressure is on her. If she doesn't win, it's a huge letdown. Everyone is mad at her. She goes from the hero to the pariah.

That's a lot of pressure. In fact, that's why it's so hard to repeat as a champion at sports. The first time, you had nothing to lose. But once you are the champion, all you can do is have it taken from you. Keeping it is twice as hard, and you are half as motivated.

I don't know about you, but in my life when I become privileged in a certain area of life, it's been a major disadvantage. I get complacent and less motivated without even thinking about it, I stop working as hard. I expect to win, and yet, there's more pressure to win. It's why I work daily to keep the underdog mindset.

It can be infuriating. This is why it's so common in sports for good teams to take the slightest hint of disrespect as a major insult, and blow it out of proportion. You'll hear them on Sportscenter, "No one believes in us!" they shout, as thousands of people cheer them on in the background.

Why?

To keep themselves from the expectation of winning. This is their subconscious at work here because they do not truly understand what you are about, and how you will want, and even fight for, an underdog mindset for life.

GOING TO HOLLYWOOD

Around the start of the Internet boom, 1993 or so, a friend and I started a website that got some traction. You know all those Instagram meme and joke accounts? It was basically that before smartphones. We had funny and gross videos, all of that stuff. We'd charge people $19 a month for access and people loved it.

One day I was in my collision repair office (yes, I fixed cars and ran an internet site from the same place) and I got this email from a name I recognized: Tommy Lee.

Yeah, it was that Tommy Lee. The drummer from Motley Crue. He was a subscriber, loved the site, and sent me a message:

"This site is cool as shit man. Keep sending me stuff!!"

I had to pinch myself, Tommy Lee sent me an email!! In the 80s and 90s Motley Crue was the shit...so this was like, the greatest thing ever for me.

Before I had time to think about it, I wrote a response:

"Hey, Tommy this is Dean, cool that you joined. Been a fan of Motley Crue for a long time.

Yo man, internet pay-per-view is going to be the biggest thing in the world. We should build a website around you and Pamela [ed note: He was married to Pamela Anderson at the time] where you and she do unique things (not porn), and just show your crazy life behind the scenes, and then sell it to people on a monthly basis. I bet people would pay at least $19 a month, probably more. Just an idea man, hit me back if you are interested in talking more about it."

I was about to hit send...and immediately felt sick to my stomach.

I mean, who was I to be talking business with one of the biggest rock stars in the world? What the hell did I know?

Then I thought about it for a second. I was a pretty successful businessman at this point, I had some resources, and I knew some things. Maybe not at his level, but hey, I wasn't a bum living on the street. And Tommy was paying for my service, and he did send me an email first. OK, maybe this wasn't totally out of line.

Then my emotions swung back the other way.

I'm fooling myself. I have this piddly little website, and

here I am trying to do a deal with Tommy Lee and Pamela Anderson? (At that time Pamela was the hottest thing since Marilyn Monroe) He's going to laugh at me and call me an idiot, just like the popular kids in high school did. And I'll deserve it. I worked on cars—who did I think I was?

I was about to hit delete...and I stopped again. I thought to myself: *What's the worst that could happen?*

What was Tommy going to do? Not invite me to the Hollywood parties I wasn't even invited to anyway? Tell me to screw off and laugh at me?

It hit me: I had nothing to lose. Worst case, I was just exactly who I was at that moment.

So I hit send.

I got up from my desk, let out a huge exhale, and honestly...I felt good about myself. Yeah, he'd probably dismiss me, but so what? I was working in my little collision shop in my small town and talking back and forth to Tommy Lee—that was cool as hell, even if nothing came of it.

I took my shot. If nothing happened, so be it. At least I tried.

I went to get an iced tea, sat back down at my desk...and Tommy had already responded:

"Holy fuck, this is an amazing idea. Send me a proposal, here's my attorney's contact info, send it to him, too, let's talk."

Holy fuck is right! What do I do now?

All the calm I'd had about trying my best and not caring if he dismissed me, that stuff went right out the window. I got super anxious—now I had to write a business proposal? How the hell do I do that?

I pounded my iced tea, brain dumped my idea in a Word doc, and sent it right away to him and his attorney, without hardly even thinking about it. I was too nervous. I knew if I thought about it, I'd never send it.

The next day, I got a call:

"Dean, this is David Rudick, I'm Tommy Lee's attorney. How'd you come up with something so ingenious?"

I can't even remember what I told him, or the rest of the conversation, I was such a nervous wreck. There I was, a nothing with dirt under my nails, talking to one of the most famous attorneys in Hollywood. But I do remember this part of the conversation:

"Dean, I want you to fly out to LA, can you swing that? Let's talk about this in person, and get it moving ASAP."

I had cars to fix, houses to remodel, and all the rest but I canceled all of it. I just said "screw it" and went all in.

Tommy was emailing me every day, David I were talking on the phone constantly, and both were really nice to me. I got someone to help me create a formal business plan, and made sure it had all the different parts of a plan, the charts and graphs and our splits, and how we would run it, and all of that. I finished it and FedExed it to Tommy and David. Then I got on a plane to LA to see David.

His office was right on Sunset Boulevard, and I knew David was a famous attorney, but I had no idea just how famous he was. His office was covered in memorabilia and pictures of him with all kinds of super famous people.

I had gotten lost in the work before getting to LA, so I didn't have time to feel anxiety then. But as I stared at pictures of the most famous people on earth, all with this lawyer I was about to meet, all that anxiety came back. I was still 26 at that point, feeling insecure and really out of my league.

Eventually the receptionist told me David was ready to see me. I walked into his office, and he was just as nice as he was on the phone.

"Dean, I have to tell you, this is impressive. Your whole proposal was great. I want to do this. Let's figure it out."

When my leg stopped shaking and I was finally able to say two coherent sentences, we started to get a dialogue going.

We talked for about forty-five minutes, hammered out a bunch of details, and he was a straight-up gentleman the whole time. Then he put his phone on speaker, dialed a number and I heard this woman pick up.

David: "Pamela, Tommy. I want you two to meet Dean."

Tommy: "What's up, man."

Pamela: "Hey, Dean!"

Holy shit. That was Pamela Anderson saying my name!

David: "Guys, this is a home run. Like, I don't know how we found this guy. This is amazing. I'm going to start formalizing the agreement. Let's do this."

Tommy: "Awesome, we're in!"

David: "Hey, do you have plans tonight? How about you do dinner with Pamela and Tommy tonight to celebrate? We'll do the four of us."

Dean: "Uh...yeah...I can do that."

He shook my hand, walked me out, and I felt like I was in a dream. I made it! I'm going to dinner with Pamela Anderson megastar, and Tommy Lee, the coolest rockstar alive!

This was my first time in LA, so I rented a convertible like a total tourist, and there I was, driving down Sunset Boulevard blasting music and smiling to the point of embarrassment. I cringe to write this now, but honestly, driving around LA in my convertible, I felt like I'd made it. I was the poor mechanic with dirt under his nails that the biggest names in Hollywood wanted to do business with me!

All that anxiety, all that fear, man, that was bullshit. *I do belong here, I am good enough!*

As I was taking in all the colors of LA in my rented car, fantasizing about which house I would buy and what restaurants I'd have private tables at when my cell phone rang; it was David.

"Hey listen, I'm sitting here with Pamela and Tommy's manager. He just wants to get clear on a few things before the meeting with you and Pamela and Tommy, could you run back over here? Won't take long."

I drove right back over, walked into the office with a newfound level of confidence and went to shake the hand of Tommy's manager.

He didn't shake my hand.

"I need to know something—how the FUCK did you get in this office?"

I was stunned. For a second, I really thought he was asking me how I physically got to the office. I was about to tell him that David's secretary gave me directions and I drove there from the airport, but that's not what he was asking.

"How the fuck did you get in here? You're some nobody from upstate New York, you didn't go to college, you got some little internet business? How much do you do, a million a year? Is that what you do? Are you a millionaire? I bet that impresses all your small town friends, doesn't it? And you think you can come in here with your bullshit idea and work with us? We don't need you."

I was stunned. Speechless. Lip quivering. Not even two minutes ago, I was the happiest I'd ever been in my life, and now here I was, in the middle of my worst nightmare. Everything I worried about, all my anxiety, all of it came flooding back.

I tried to answer, but all I could do was stutter out a few choppy phrases, *"I'm sorry...I know it's just a little site...but I have the merchant account connections...you can just judge it on the merits...I have all the video streaming technology already set up...I can make this work, it's already working on my site..."*

He cut me off, "Yeah, the idea may be good. So, then why the hell would we do this with you? You don't think we got better connections than you? You're going to have to leave. We'll talk to you tomorrow."

David said to me, "Dean, during the dinner with Tommy and Pamela tonight—"

The manager barked at him, "There's no fucking dinner! I canceled that already. Goodbye, Dean."

I went back to my hotel room, and for three hours, I did nothing but cry. I heaved and sobbed and cried like I was dying. And honestly, part of me felt like I had died.

I couldn't sleep a wink that night. All night, between my sobs, all my negative self-talk came back. Who the hell did I think I was? He's right. I am just a nobody from Marlboro, New York. I'm just a dreamer like so many people have accused me of being in the past. I don't belong out here. I should never have let this happen.

David called me the next morning, apologized, and told me what I already knew: the deal was off. I got on the next plane back to New York, and slunk home.

Believe it or not, it actually got worse.

I got off the plane from California, tail between my legs, feeling pathetic. After a full day of travel, I finally got back to my place late at night. My answering machine was going crazy with messages. One of my apartment houses had a literal sewage explosion.

There was an issue with the septic tank being clogged and all the waste from the three stories above it dumped into one little bathroom. The sewage was literally knee-high in his bathroom, and of course, he's calling me screaming that there's shit all over his house.

I called everyone I knew, and no one—not a single plumber or handyman—was available late on a Saturday night.

So I went over there and started shoveling shit into a spackling bucket—what else could I do? I had my fishing waders, no exaggeration, and a painting mask, shoveling raw sewage for three hours on a Saturday night.

I have had some low moments in my life, but that might be one of the worst.

UNDERDOGS HAVE NOTHING TO LOSE (AND CAN USE THIS TO DO ANYTHING)

Everyone looks at all the advantages that the so-called privileged have and miss the massive advantage that the underdog has:

When you have nothing to lose, you can do anything you want.

You have no risk. When no one expects you to do anything, then you can do everything.

As an underdog, you almost can't lose. All you have to do is try, because even the attempt is better than you were before.

Underdogs can take risks, they can experiment, they can try and fail, because who cares if they lose? It doesn't matter. It's ALL upside.

This is not unique to me. Lots of underdogs do it. One of my favorite examples is the actor, Danny Trejo. You most likely know him without realizing it, he's the super tough-looking guy in every movie.

Danny was a bigger underdog than me. He grew up as a child drug addict and criminal, in and out of prison for years. While serving time in San Quentin, he competed in and won the prison boxing title. He got out, cleaned himself up in a twelve-step program, and began to sponsor other guys. One of the guys he sponsored was an actor, and had an emergency on a movie set. Danny rushed to his aid, and the director was so impressed with Danny's appearance and manner, he offered Danny a role as an extra in the movie.

It gets better. The director learned of Trejo's boxing skills and paid him to train the actors for a boxing match that was later in the movie. And he did so well training the actors that he re-cast Danny as the main competitor for the lead actor in the boxing match.

Now, think about this: Danny was the furthest thing from a Hollywood actor. He had no business on a movie set. He knew this, so he just had fun with it and tried his best. And because he had nothing to lose, he ended up doing a great job...and became one of the most iconic character actors in America today.

I now look for ways to constantly put myself back in the mindset of an underdog, even though in so many ways that is not what I am at all. I put myself in that state of mind because it frees me up to do what I know I have to do to succeed: take risks, be free, explore, and just have fun because everything is a bonus.

Underdogs have nothing to lose.

Underdogs have no one to impress.

Underdogs have no expectations to meet.

Underdogs have nowhere to go but up.

I'm telling you, as a guy who has been at the lowest lows you can get to, and some of the highest highs, I actually did some of my best work when I was down and out and no one expected anything from me.

When I had nothing to lose, I felt free to be who I really was.

HOW HOLLYWOOD TAUGHT ME I HAD NOTHING TO LOSE

The whole time I was shoveling that shit in my rental house, I was thinking to myself, "I guess this is where I deserved to be. This is just a sign from God, obviously."

That's the stuff that you think about in moments like that, don't you?

But as I thought that, it started to get better. My self-talk changed, "You know what, I'm successful. I own several apartment houses. Yeah, I'm cleaning shit out of one of them, but I still own them. I'm not poor, I'm not broke."

Several months later, I saw that they launched the site on their own. They took my idea, down to every detail, and did it themselves. Pamela was on Jay Leno, she was talking about it, and she was using the exact language I'd written in my proposal about what she'd say on his show.

I got sick. Literally sick to my stomach. She was considered by many to be one of the hottest women on earth, and I couldn't even look at Pamela as she said my words. It hurt me on a deep level, and it brought back my insecurities.

I thought to myself, "I reached my plateau. I tried to go to California with the big boys. I stepped off the path, got bit by a snake. I can just get back on the path. I'm a car guy who does houses, and that's OK."

Of course, the site failed. They took the concept, but messed up all the details. Most importantly, they missed the relationship aspect between Tommy and Pamela that was the whole key to the site. Basically, I envisioned this concept as having the intimacy and drama of reality TV before it was really a thing, and they didn't get any of that.

Like I said, there's no happy ending to this part of the story. I didn't do the site later on. I've still never met Tommy and Pamela. I never got into Hollywood. At that moment in time this episode was a failure in my life.

Unless you look at it in the context of my whole life.

I don't remember if it was two weeks or two months, but for a while, I said to myself that I just needed to do what I do best—cars and real estate.

And I did that. I pulled back on my ambitions. And I was cool with it. In fact, it was me pulling back that taught me one of the most important Underdog Advantages: I learned I had nothing to lose by trying.

Yeah, this episode hurt, and yeah, it knocked me down. But when I got back home, I still had my houses and my car business.

But after a few months, I learned that *I hadn't actually lost anything.* The only thing I "lost" was a deal I never actually had. And yeah, that made me feel really bad about myself, but that was just my ego. I realized that I felt bad about myself generally, and that by having Hollywood "accept me," it made me feel important. It gave me significance.

But the more I thought about it, the more I realized that Hollywood couldn't tell me who I was. So what that they didn't want me? That doesn't make me a bad person, or less, or anything.

Think about it: what was the only thing that I actually risked?

The feeling of importance and significance I would have gotten from being in Hollywood and working with Tommy and Pamela.

OK, yeah, I did risk that. And yeah, I did feel bad about myself when I got rejected.

But once I got past that, I realized that I had it all wrong. I stopped looking at the whole event as something that would have given me significance if I had gotten the deal; instead, I saw myself as having significance simply because I took the shot! And when I looked around, I didn't see anyone else I knew going after it like I was.

In fact, the more distance I got from the incident, the more proud of myself I was. I mean, I came from nowhere and almost signed a huge deal with some of the biggest stars on earth. How cool is that? Yeah, I didn't get it, but so what? If I could get that close now, with no experience or connections, think of what I can do when I get some more experience!

Looking back, this failure was one of the best things to ever happen to me. If I hadn't done this, if I hadn't taken this risk—and failed—I think I would have quit what ended up becoming the thing that launched me into the self-education world: Motor Millions (I'll tell that story later). And the only reason I kept going with Motor Millions is because *I knew I had nothing to lose.*

To share a little update on this story...many years later I got a call out of nowhere. I picked up the phone, and the caller said:

David: "Dean? This is David Rudich."

Dean: "David, oh my god! I can hear your name now and not be sick to my stomach."

David: "Ah, that's funny. So sorry all that happened. I just wanted to tell you I've been following your success and I'm really proud of you. I had no doubts about where you were going. I wish it hadn't gone the way it did, but I'm thinking maybe it happened exactly the way it was supposed to."

Dean: "Thank you, David, that means a lot to me."

David: "How about you come out to L.A.? I'd love to catch up with you."

I flew out to LA. I went to his office with a completely new perspective. I walked through that door not feeling intimidated anymore. Now I felt accomplished. We embraced and caught up and jumped in his Range Rover and he drove me to his house, and then drove me to property that he owned on top of the Hollywood Hills that used to be owned by a prince, and asked for my advice on what he should do with that property.

It was at that moment I realized that it was all part of the plan. It was part of paying my success tax. It was part of building the grit, the muscle it takes to be successful. It was a part of learning how to take underdog disadvantages, and make them empowering advantages in my life.

UNDERDOG CHALLENGE #1

What's a story in your life that has been an anchor for you? The story of "Why it didn't happen." The story of whose fault it was that you didn't reach that plateau, make it happen, get the deal, or get the desired outcome.

No matter how awful or horrific or regretful that story is, how can you take a moment right now and reframe or retell that story, and see it through a different lens?

What if that horrible event was actually designed for you by God, or the universe (or whatever you believe in) to get you to this point right now? What if life happened for you, not to you (as Tony Robbins likes to say)?

What if this so-called failure, loss, or pain was actually the ingredient to the greatest version of you?

How did you come out stronger, better, wiser? How can that event allow you to become braver and more capable?

To recap:

What's the story that's holding you back?

What could you have actually learned from it?

Take the power away from the negative thoughts regarding that story, prove it's a lie, get mad that it has held you back even this long.

Then reframe that story so it becomes the wind behind your sail, not an anchor holding you back.

What's the new story?

CHAPTER 2

Underdogs Can Use "The Power of You Can't"

The best thing that can happen to me is when someone tells me I can't do something.

Yes, you read that right.

I love it when people doubt me.

I wasn't always like this. I used to hate it when people told me I couldn't do something. I would get sad and lose my confidence and in many cases assume they were right.

It was my Uncle Larry who finally showed me what I now call, "The Power of You Can't."

From my earliest memories, I remember my great Uncle Larry asking me what I wanted to do after college. My reply, for years, had been, "I am not going to college, I am going to start my own business and be a millionaire so I can take care of my Mom."

That's exactly what I said every time. And he would have the same half-ass sarcastic, patronizing reply, "Ah, isn't that cute, but that's not the way it works Dean. You'll realize that soon enough."

Over the years he'd been lecturing me about going to college, and to be honest, it wore me down. It was always sorta depressing because, quite honestly, I sucked at school and I hated it. I was in the special ed reading class for god's sake, how would I ever go to college? I always left discussions with him feeling a little bit like a loser.

Well, this one time, things were different. I was probably fifteen or so and feeling a little bit of confidence. I'd been working with my dad every day at his auto body shop, and I learned some things about business. My drive for success was off the charts and I was finding new ways to move forward faster than expected. I'd come up with some ways for the business to be more organized and run faster, I'd made some money, and I realized I was pretty decent at it. I saw a future there.

Uncle Larry started in again, "Well, Dean, you're getting older. What are you thinking about doing for work?"

"I think I might go into business with my Dad and then

branch into real estate. I think I could make some good money there."

Excited about sharing, I launched into my ideas for making my Dad's collision shop way more profitable, and how I was going to buy my first house with no money down, and then he stopped me short.

"Oh, so what college will you learn business at?"

"I don't think I'm going to college. I'm not that smart and I can learn this on my own, it's not so hard."

"Well then Dean, I think your father is doing you a big disservice by letting you have these pie-in-the-sky dreams because they simply aren't going to happen. You have to go to college or you'll be stuck in a career you hate."

Usually, him telling me that would ding my confidence and state of mind.

But this time was different.

I don't know why, and I didn't say it out loud to him at the time, but I remember thinking, for the first time:

Uncle Larry, you have no idea what you are talking about. You're flat-out wrong.

First off, he and my Aunt Mary were always tight on cash. I

remember my grandmother helping them out a few times. How had going to college helped him, if he couldn't even provide for his family at the level he desired?

Second, he worked for someone else. That was surely NEVER an option for me. I was going to own my own business.

And looking through the eyes of a fifteen-year-old I remember thinking: his car sucks. I wouldn't drive it if you paid me.

As I thought about this, I don't know where this came from—I got pissed at him.

Who the hell was he to tell me what I could and could not do?

I swore, then and there, that I was going to prove him wrong. That I not only wasn't going to college, but I was going to make a bunch of money, and have a better car, and a better house, and a better life than he had.

And in that moment, I learned the advantage that has helped fuel me so many times in my life: underdogs have lots of sources for motivation and maybe the biggest one in your life that you're not seeing is what I like to call, "The Power of You Can't."

THE PRIVILEGED STRUGGLE TO KEEP MOTIVATED

When you get to the top, when you win the championship, when you make your first million, you celebrate.

And you should. You earned it.

There's a problem though. For most privileged people— those who either never had underdog roots, or forget the power of the underdog mindset—that celebration marks the end. They almost never stay on top.

They fall off just as quick as they get to the top.

This is because they don't have the grit, the skills, and the habits to sustain their success. They don't have the experience and the history of fighting. They haven't battled their whole life to "win." They are the privileged, they win yeah, but in many cases it simply doesn't last.

But here's the thing: it's not just their skills. If they had the skills to get to the top, then it's possible for them to figure out how to stay there. But they don't stay on the top of the mountain because they are missing a huge piece of sustainable success.

What they are missing is inner, driving, and ongoing motivation. They are missing the underdog state of mind.

When you get to the top and you become privileged, everyone celebrates you. Everyone wants to associate with you. You're a winner. It's great.

The problem with this is that now no one tells you the truth. Everyone thinks, because you're the winner, that you are amazing and nothing you do is wrong. They stop telling you the truth.

This might sound cool, but it's a disaster in the making. It's a funny thing—the more successful you become, the less attached to reality you are, but the more necessary it is to know the reality of the situation so you can stay on top.

This has happened to hundreds of bands. It's why there are so many "one-hit wonders" in music. Once you break through, and have a big hit, you become the privileged. You lose the motivation, "the underdog hunger," and the focus that got you there.

This is such a cliché that the bands that have sustained success are actually much more rare than the ones that pop up, do well, and then fall away. The Rolling Stones have had forty years of success, but for every band like them, there are literally thousands of Dexys Midnight Runners (Google that all you millennials, you'll love it).

It's a cliché in sports for teams to use "No one believes in us!" as their battle cry because it happens so often. Without

Underdog Hunger to push them, the privileged almost inevitably lose their edge. They become soft and complacent.

"NO, YOU CAN'T RACE AGAINST THEM."

When I was twenty years old, I bought a brand-new Polaris 650 triple cylinder snowmobile, one of the fastest production snowmobiles at the time. It was over $5,000. I financed it for a $197 per month payment and was super excited.

I'm an adrenaline junkie, so I decided to race it. I wanted to modify it to make it even faster. The problem: I had no money to do that. I couldn't hire anyone to rebuild the engine or add any cool aftermarket parts or anything like that at all.

So, being the resourceful underdog that I was, I started doing a lot of research. I found out the best way to put spikes in the tracks so it would grab and grip faster. I found a way to adjust the suspension so it was hard and strong and not too bouncy, so the front end wouldn't go up. I found a way to adjust the clutching and the gears to my weight so it shifted quicker, and increase the speed significantly without spending thousands of dollars.

So, in my little town of Marlborough, New York, I became the king of the snowmobile races. No one beat me and people came from miles away to try.

It was awesome. They'd pull up with their fancy trailers, and I'd just get excited—because I'd pull up with my pickup truck with a box of tools and drag my snowmobile off my pickup truck and race these guys that spent way more money on their snowmobiles than I did.

But that was only for fun at an old airport where people met on Sundays whenever there was snow on the ground. One day after winning about fifteen races in a row, someone said, "Why don't you race professionally? They have whole leagues for this."

I had no idea. I was only racing against hobbyists, like me. So I said what the heck? I called and registered, then drove about two hours the following Saturday to my first event. I got third place out of the gate. I raced against people that were way more advanced than me and doing really well with a lot more money, and I got third place.

I was completely hooked. I wanted to race for real against the professionals.

Here was the problem: My funds were extremely limited. I had no connections. I wasn't a snowmobile mechanic, I had no business racing against people who did this for a living, and who had access to the resources the pros had.

My local snowmobile dealer said, "Oh, on that small little circuit you raced at, you had a chance. But you can't go to the bigger brackets because you'll be going against the big boys like Team Arctic Cat, Team Yamaha, Team Ski-Doo, Team Polaris. You're going to race against sponsored racers who get all of their stuff for free. They pretty much have unlimited money and resources at their disposal. They have the latest, the greatest, they have replacement motors, replacement clutches. They have a team of five, maybe even seven people. They show up in their beautiful tractor-trailers, lower the back gate and you drool over how pristine everything is." I could feel his envy or maybe a bad experience in his words. Then he ended with, "That's not a bracket for you. But you can have lots of fun in the bracket you raced in, with hobbyists like you, stick to that."

By then, I had already mastered the art of saying, "Fuck that" to the people who told me "you can't."

Now that seems harsh. So let me be clear. That was not an FU to the local snowmobile dealer. Dave was a great guy. No, it was more to the concept of flipping off anything that was supposedly out of my league and I could not try. It was becoming a really strong underdog advantage for me by then and I was harnessing that power any way I could.

So no, I did not have the money, the resources, the connections, or even believers.

But I had something most of them didn't: I was resourceful and was hell-bent on figuring it out.

UNDERDOGS CAN FIND MOTIVATION EVERYWHERE

When my team and I were doing some research, we polled 25,000 people who had bought a real estate course from me, and asked if they weren't already making the money they desired, what was the number one thing they felt was holding them back from being financially successful.

I thought they would say things like, "Not enough time in my life." Or "Your education isn't detailed enough."

Almost no one said that. But there was one overwhelming response:

Forty-two percent said that negative people in their lives held them back. This was the number one response by almost half.

If you go look at my social media posts, people say things like this all the time:

"I'd love to do this but my husband thinks I'm crazy to be an entrepreneur."

"My parents told me I'm not doing this."

"My brother says I'm an idiot."

Everybody feels the negativity around them, and they see this as a major impediment to their success.

But what if this was actually an underdog advantage? What if you could use this negativity to push yourself forward?

In my life, the best successes have always been after people told me these things:

"You can't do that."

"No one could pull that off."

"Stop being a dreamer."

"That takes more money than you have to make it work."

Now, I use these statements as fuel to push me through all the hard parts.

When you're an underdog, it doesn't take a lot of work to get started. It's usually pretty easy to make some progress. You have a lot of advantages that will help you (as detailed in the other chapters).

But underdogs do have to deal with naysayers, and they are usually their friends or family. These are the people who probably mean well, but the fact is, they never did anything with their lives, and watching you succeed makes them think about the things they wished they did—but didn't.

That's why they are telling you that you can't do it. Everyone has a dream, and most people discard it. And when anyone stands up and has the gall to try and reach their dream, so many people will consciously or subconsciously try and pull them back.

Either they're afraid that you will fail and they care about you, or they are envious that you have the courage to reach for and achieve your dreams—and sometimes it's both.

This is such an advantage when people do this—it creates motivation and fuel. Do you know how many things that are integral to our society were called crazy and impossible when they first came out?

The *New York Sun* said this about bicycles, "As a fad cycling is dead, and few individuals now ride for all the good they claim to see in the pastime when it was fashion."

Here's what the *New York Times* said about the car, "Automobiling is following the history of cycling with such remarkable closeness in almost every detail, both as a sport and an industry, that the question is often asked if the present period of expansion will be followed by a collapse as complete and as disastrous as was that of the cycling boom of a few short years ago."

What's so crazy is that the head of IBM didn't think computers would ever catch on! Thomas Watson said, "I think there is a world market for maybe five computers."

And it's not inventions either. One of the greatest entrepreneurs of the twenty-first century is Jack Ma, the man who started Alibaba. Listening to his story humbles me.

He failed in his primary school examinations (which are like the SATs of China) not once, but twice. And then to make it worse, he failed his middle school exams three times. Then he failed his university exams three times.

After school, he had the hardest time getting a job. Before he started Alibaba, he was rejected from forty-three jobs, including at Kentucky Fried Chicken! He said, "When KFC came to my town in China, twenty-four people went for the job. Twenty-three people were accepted. I was the only guy who wasn't."

Can you imagine being the only guy that KFC won't hire??

If failure and the finger pointing can be used as motivation, no wonder he started one of the most successful companies of all times.

But naysayers and haters aren't the only sources of motivation. There are two other sources that underdogs can use very easily: heartbreak and disappointment.

No one likes to be in pain. No one wants to suffer. No one likes feeling let down.

But we all go through this. So why not use it?

In fact, I think this is an underestimated underdog advantage that when used properly is jet fuel.

Heartbreak is going to cause anguish. You can use it, or you can let it use you. We really are the ones in control of that choice.

THE NEW ENGLAND STATE SNOWMOBILE CHAMPION

Now don't get me wrong: having minimal money, no resources and no sponsors was a serious obstacle. I had to figure out a way around this.

So I started asking everybody I could. I'd literally cold call people that were professional mechanics for snowmobiles, and I'd say, "Listen, I'd love to give you the business to redo my snowmobile, but if I did, what would you do?"

And sometimes I'd get a great person on the phone, and they'd tell me everything, "Hey, let me just tell you, son. If you don't have the money to do a complete modification, try this: try grinding your weights, try changing the angles so the trajectory is different. Try this gear ratio."

They would literally just tell me all these cool tricks to try. So after a few months of calling every snowmobile mechanic I could find, I had an incredible list of things to test out.

So I got my tools, and I got a little file, and some extra clutch weights and I went out in the apple orchard by my house. I marked off 500 feet, handed my Dad or a friend a stopwatch and said, "Time me."

I'd go full speed for the 500 ft and have them time it and mark it down. Then I would make a tweak or two and go again seeing if I could beat the prior time. Again and again. Adjustment after adjustment.

I'd change the gear ratio. I'd adjust the clutches. I'd file the weights. I'd put a different belt on. I'd hook up a cooling system on it. All with the desire to cut time on that 500-foot race.

The whole time, I was just fueled by "the power of you can't" and I was thinking "just because they're sponsored by Team Yamaha or Team Arctic Cat or Team Ski-Doo or Team Polaris, they aren't better than me."

I specifically remember when I got to my first race, driving past and then parking next to all the other racers with my older pickup truck, lugging my snowmobile off the back of the truck, grabbing my tools that were in an old milk crate, and feeling like they were looking at me and laughing.

Whether they were or they weren't didn't matter. It was my fuel. I remember thinking in my head, not with a chip, but as my confidence builder, "The hell with you all, go ahead and laugh now. We'll see what happens in the race."

I raced in the 650cc class. Then they had an 800cc class, which was a much bigger machine. Then they had an Open "Mod" class. Meaning there were 1000cc snowmobiles, much bigger than mine, modified out to the max, and wow, they were so crazy loud. I threw all caution to the wind and entered all three of those racing brackets.

I took first place in the 650cc, took first place in the 800cc, and took third place in the Open. In fact, I beat everybody so pathetically bad that they protested and they literally tore my machine down.

Meaning, they took the motor apart to see if I was cheating, see if it was actually a 1000cc engine and I had lied.

And there wasn't one thing wrong with it.

Everybody was in shock and could not understand how this little 650cc machine, coming from this guy with a pickup truck and a milk crate of old tools, could beat them.

Because of my age and lack of life experience—I didn't realize at the time—I was becoming more and more resourceful, fueled by this underdog advantage. I was being driven when seemingly privileged folks told me I couldn't, because the world told me I couldn't, because I didn't have money, and I took all that and turned the power of you can't into the power of "Hell yes I can!"

I ended up going almost three years without losing one race on the pro circuit. It all culminated at the New England Championship (for people outside the country, New England is Connecticut, New Jersey, New York, Massachusetts, and New Hampshire).

This was a big deal. I was racing against the biggest teams in the country. Team Ski-Doo, Team Arctic Cat, all of them. There, where the beautiful tractor-trailers with team names on the side of them lined up, where each person would have an extra snowmobile, they had pit crews, it was unlike anything I'd seen. It was like a NASCAR race for snowmobiles.

I pulled up with two of my buddies in my Toyota pickup truck with my five-year-old snowmobile in the back. I have to admit I was a little hungover because I went out the night before with my buddies to celebrate a birthday, ended up having a great time, and stayed out way too late.

So picture this, I showed up hungover with my tools still in a milk crate. I had jeans on and Timberland work boots with paint stains on them. I could feel people giving me the,

"Why the hell is that guy even here?" look. And by this time in my life, I loved it.

And because I wasn't nationally ranked and didn't have a team, I had to qualify to be in the final match. I had to race four or five times before I even got into the final. I won two or three races and one of the guy's dads came up to me and said, "Hey, congratulations for getting this far, but you've only raced against the shitty people. Be prepared because you haven't got to these guys yet," and he pointed to the big sponsored team trucks. "They race last."

He said, "But I want to give you credit son, you came a long way for having an old machine and no crew, you've come a long way."

And though I remember him being really nice and he probably wasn't being mean, I remember thinking, "Fuck that."

Here's the thing. It didn't make me mad. It made me inspired.

That sobered me up right away. I did everything in my power. I went and sanded down my clutch so it wasn't so smooth, so the belt would stick stronger when I slammed on the gas. I cooled the machine, I got in the right mindset because the nanosecond the light turns green, you must hit the gas or the pros will jump out way ahead of you. If you ever watch drag racing, it goes red, red, red, yellow, green, and you hit the gas.

My timing was perfect. I practiced that timing over and over. I used to have a handlebar in my room, and I'd practice my timing over and over. Heck, I'd practice it hundreds and hundreds of times.

So I got to that final heat; I made it all the way to the championship race where I was up against Team Arctic Cat, Team Ski-Doo, and all the rest of the badasses who made it that far. Just to be in that lineup was an amazing feat. I was the only non-team person who made it to the final, and I got up to the light, my heart beating through my fucking chest. I remember looking at all of them and not disliking them, just saying, "You don't know who I am. I got this. You think I can't. Look at me as if I have no chance, please underestimate me, I can't wait."

And that light turned green, and I got out of the gate first. Three of them were right next to me, team Ski-Doo looked like they would pass me and it was like my snowmobile had the same "it ain't happening" desires I did. The snowmobile track caught a groove and my machine sped up, and I passed across the finish line inches in front of the number two racer. I took first place and became the New England State Champion in the 650 class.

And the 750 class.

All with a 650 engine.

And I never would have gotten there if I hadn't been an underdog, and had "The Power of You Can't" pushing me from behind.

UNDERDOG CHALLENGE #2

So now, how does this relate to you? Let's get disturbed. Yes, more often than not, action comes from being disturbed.

When in the past did you come up with an idea, a concept, an invention? Maybe something you thought the world would want to buy on TV or online?

Maybe you told some friends, or family members. Maybe your father, your mother, your husband, your wife, someone you trust. And what happened? They gave you twenty reasons why it would never work. They said things like, "People already thought about it," "You'd have to get a trademark," "Takes money to do things like that," "You'd have to get it made in China." Or the killer one, "If it was going to be successful, somebody would have already done it."

Maybe you didn't cave immediately, but it was enough of

those people telling you, "You can't," that it flipped the scales in the direction of non-action, and you continued on the path you were on. And then, a year or two later, someone else took your idea? Or that same idea was on TV, online, or in stores, making someone else millions of dollars.

I challenge you to stop for a moment and truly think about the pain of the time you missed out, when you felt left behind, when someone else capitalized on something you had already thought of, and how bad that felt.

Yes, I want to cause a little pain so you'll take this challenge seriously and take action right now. I want you to realize you are being held back by the power of other people telling you that you can't.

As simple as it sounds what could be holding you back is simply the opinions and thoughts from people who are unqualified to tell you no. You are allowing a belief created in someone else's mind to hold you back from reaching new heights.

So, in this challenge, I would love for you to recognize who they are and what they're saying.

Who told you that you can't?

Are they qualified to tell you?

Are they telling you because they want to protect you?

Are they telling you because they might be envious that you'll try something, and maybe get ahead of them?

If they're doing that, it's not on purpose. It's their subconscious thinking they're protecting you—when they're really protecting themselves.

So, how can you take this challenge and use those people telling you that you can't and allow that to fuel your drive?

Not to fuel you to do stupid things, not to fuel you to do things without research, without having a path and a plan— but how can we shift that today to be your motivation? To be your inspiration?

Take the time to think about regrets in the past of listening to the wrong words and how you could take the present and make the power of "you can't" your underdog advantage.

Think about how, someday when you look back and you tell your children, your grandchildren, the story of when the world doubted you, when your family doubted you, how you used their power as fuel to break through to the best version of yourself.

CHAPTER 3

Underdogs Act Fast and Improve Quickly

I beat the hell out of three ex-NFL players.

At a sport.

OK...it was fishing.

But still, it was an actual physical activity that we competed at outdoors.

It happened when I was invited to a mastermind with a bunch of good friends and influencers you may know. People like Lewis Howes, Tom Bilyeu, Jeff Walker, Russell Brunson, Brendon Burchard, Dave Holis, Anthony Trucks, Trent Shelton, and several other amazing people. We planned on masterminding in the Idaho mountains and in our free time, get in some fly fishing at my dear friend Randy Garn's trout ranch.

This trip was off the charts amazing and it was all frickin' men. Just pure testosterone. Even better? Three of them, Lewis, Anthony, and Trent all played in the NFL. So this was not just all dudes, it was a straight up "pretend we aren't in competition for everything even though we are" long weekend of fun and learning. Who got the best room in the lodge, who ate the most steak, who got up earlier, ran the mountain in the best time, and all the rest as you can imagine.

It was a blast. The learning from each other, the outdoors, the breakthroughs came together magically and yes, the unspoken competition was building up until it was time for an actual challenge with teams and prizes. Well, mostly bragging rights.

The competition was fishing. The cool part was I didn't have to be six-feet-plus and look like a Greek God to compete. Yes I stay in shape, but I'm no Anthony Trucks, who also competed in and won *American Ninja Warrior* on TV. In fishing, thankfully those assets really don't matter.

So I used one of the most important underdog advantages, the one that has helped me at every stage of my life: I acted fast, learned from my successes and failures, and used them to improve rapidly.

THE PRIVILEGED HAVE TO PLAN THEIR ACTIONS CAREFULLY

When you are at the top of your game and everyone knows it, you have to be careful. You have a target on your back because everyone wants to be you, to take your spot. Yes, they are judging everything you do.

You can't just try new things because everyone is watching. As brutal as this may sound, if you mess something up, in more cases than we would like to believe, people see it and think less of you.

Because of this, you have to plan your moves carefully. You have to make sure you know exactly what you're doing before you do it. You have to take into consideration what others' perceptions of your actions are, and most importantly, you have to ensure that everything you do is or at least looks like "the right thing." Testing new methods, trying new things, just having fun—that's not as easy anymore. In many cases there is just too much at stake.

This means that action can take a long time to get done, sometimes years. And that action is now designed by committee, subject to review at every level.

Remember New Coke? If you're a millennial, you probably haven't heard of this, but in 1985 there was NOTHING bigger than Coke. I know now you go to a convenience store and there are 100 flavors of everything, but back then, there was Coke and Pepsi (and a few people liked 7up) and that was it.

Coke, feeling the pressure from Pepsi right on their heels, decided to change their flavor. They called the new flavor New Coke. They made a huge deal out of this, I mean it was THE story in the media that year.

And it totally bombed. People hated it.

And it took Coke by complete surprise. I mean, they had tested this new flavor for many years. The data was clear: people liked the taste more. Everyone said that.

But they didn't think about all the emotional attachment people had to Coke; the committee just made the "right" decisions (at least, right by the standards of the privileged at the time).

And it took forever for Coke to admit they were wrong and scrap New Coke entirely, hurting their bottom line deeply. They had to come out with "Coke Classic" and sell it alongside New Coke, and then eventually they quietly retired New Coke ten years later.

The privileged also have problems learning from mistakes and improving rapidly. When you're at the top, everyone has an opinion about what you should and shouldn't do. Those opinions become deafening and overwhelming.

And often, people don't even truly understand how or why they succeeded in the first place. Success is a very poor teacher—it only teaches you to repeat what you've already done. Well, what happens when that stops working, and you have to try something else? It's not so easy once you have already told yourself that a certain set of beliefs are why you succeeded. It forces you to totally re-examine your beliefs, which most people don't want to do. It's too threatening. It can compromise their entire identity.

You remember Blackberry? They were so important to the American business person they were literally called "crackberries." The original Blackberry was a smartphone, with an actual keyboard on it, so typing was easier for people. They were revolutionary in the 90s, because the on-screen displays weren't good yet and it was the only way to access and send email effectively from a phone. But then the iPhone came out. And Blackberry refused to change—they were the privileged and didn't feel they had to. Now, you have to google them to even see a picture of one of their phones. All in about ten years time they went from hero to zero.

The privileged also have a hard time improving. Once you are at the top of your game, how do you go up? There is a reason that so few sports teams repeat in championships—once they win, they aren't hungry anymore, and they rest on their laurels. They don't dive deep and keep improving. That's why teams like the Golden State Warriors and New England Patriots are so remarkable—because they are the rare exception of champions who keep their underdog mindset alive even after holding that trophy high in the air year after year.

It's hard to improve when you are the best. How do you know who to measure yourself against? What do you use as your fuel when you are already at the top?

A real statistic is that almost everyone who gets to the top doesn't stay—because they stop doing the things that underdogs do that got them to the top (like moving fast and learning from mistakes). The best example of this is the stock market. Did you know that in 1965, the average time a company would spend on the S&P 500 was thirty-three years? By 1990, it was twenty years. It's forecast to shrink to fourteen years by 2026!

Everyone thinks they want to be the top dog, but they don't really understand how hard it is once you get there. How stuck you become, how hard it is to make progress, how learning and improving becomes exponentially harder, and how easy it is to stall and fail.

As they say, when you are at the top, the only place to go is down. Except those who truly understand how to carry the underdog mindset with them through their entire lifetime and career.

FISHING WITH COMPETITORS

We got set up to trout fish and we were paired up in twos (I got paired with Lewis Howes). There were eight different spots to fish. There was a guide at each station, and each pair got twenty-five minutes at each of the eight fishing holes. They gave us a quick lesson, our little card to write down the type, size, and quantity of the trout we caught (and released) and then we were set up to start.

This was the main competition of the weekend. All the other nonsense was small-time—whoever caught the most fish, the biggest fish, and the most variety won.

After Lewis realized we were chosen as partners, he literally grabbed and hugged me to where my feet came off the ground. After a high five and a few "Woooot Woooots," there may have been a little taunting of "You guys are finished, winners right here."

Trent is a quiet killer. Probably the way he was when he played under Peyton Manning on the Colts. He just looked at us, said nothing but I know he was thinking..."Keep talking boys, my partner and I are going to do this."

Anthony Trucks and all the others each had their own way of humbly peacocking and sharing their excitement, since each of these successful entrepreneurs and competitors figured, "I'm winning this."

The truth is, I kept a straight face and even-keeled emotions and said nothing. I wished them all luck...and smiled wide, because I had something none of them knew about: A massive underdog advantage.

UNDERDOGS CAN TAKE ACTION, LEARN FROM IT, AND IMPROVE RAPIDLY

When you are an underdog, it's a massive advantage—you are free to take lots of action, make mistakes, learn from them, and improve rapidly.

To me, this is possibly the best thing about being an underdog, and it's why I work so hard to keep myself in an underdog mindset:

Underdogs can be humble learners, and use that to propel themselves to success.

My favorite examples are comedians. Take Tiffany Haddish for example. She is a huge comedian. Her tours pack venues around the country, months in advance. She's also an in-demand movie star, who gets millions to be in a movie. Every media outlet wants to talk to her.

But do you know how she develops her comedy material?

She shows up to open mics at tiny, no-name comedy clubs, without announcing herself to the audience, and gets up and does her experimental bits.

This woman gets paid BIG dollars to headline a comedy—why is she appearing for free, next to a bunch of amateurs, with often only a few dozen people in the audience?

Because every (good) comedian does this when they are testing new material. They humble themselves, they go in front of regular people—small crowds are better—and they try new things. They often bomb jokes. Or screw up delivery. Or get timing wrong. And yes, they get booed.

They make adjustments on the fly. Learn from what's working and quickly figure out what is a dud. And that is how they create great sets.

By spending the time to test a ton of material over and over, they can make the needed adjustments. And that is why Tiffany packs huge concert halls and has tons of movie offers—because even though she's privileged now, she still trains like an underdog.

I do the same thing (sort of). You may follow me on social media, or YouTube, or be on my email list. If you do, then you know I post a lot. What you probably don't know is that I read thousands of comments every month.

Let me say that again: I literally read thousands of comments every single month on all the different platforms.

Fortunately, 98 percent of them are amazing, inspire me, and give me fuel to keep pushing forward and delivering value. But I'm sure you know, some of them are mean and nasty!

So why do I do that? Why spend the time and sometimes even be upset by the comment section on the social media platforms?

Because those are people like you. People I am trying to help, and how else can I know what they think or how they are suffering if I'm not listening to them? People will tell you exactly how they need help, if you stop and really listen to them—so I do.

In fact, I have to read the comments, because at this stage in my life, I'm not an underdog anymore. I have a huge house. I stay in fancy hotels. I fly in private jets. My kids are thriving. Business is growing like mad. So I can't sit here and pretend that my life sucks. It doesn't. I really love my life.

But if I want to keep succeeding, keep achieving, and keep

impacting lives, I have to put myself back into the underdog mindset continuously. It's truly an unfair advantage of mine. Because know for an absolute fact that when I am in that mindset I take faster action and that means I can learn from mistakes and then fuel the wins at a pace most people and competitors can't compete with.

At this stage, most every action I take is watched by millions of people and the comments keep rolling in. It can be tough at times, when you don't get the reactions you were going for or even worse, seeing my mistakes thrown back into my face.

But when I look at this through the eyes of an underdog, can you see how it is such an advantage?

When you're an underdog, it's really easy to take action and make mistakes. Very few people are watching. The stakes are really low. There's virtually no risk.

Because of this, underdogs can try so many things at a faster pace, and they can see very quickly what works and what doesn't. Then they can do more of what works, and less of what doesn't. Seems so basic, but I am telling you, this is revolutionary for most people. Most people just do the same thing over and over and never change. How is never changing going to get you anything except what you already have? It won't!

Another thing that's fun about being an underdog is that it's so easy to make progress. You have so many things you can do, so much to fix and improve, that the progress is exponential. I can remember back when I was struggling to succeed, and it really was much easier to get momentum. The rapid growth I had when I was just doing cars and real estate was because I was doing it so wrong at first, each little positive move gave me huge lifts in success and revenue. There was so much room to improve and so little competition, that getting some success was simple. Every step up you take, the improvements get a little harder.

I know this sounds crazy but as I write this, it's clear that the worse off your life is, the easier it is to make your life better. At this point in my life, and in NO WAY am I complaining, it takes a lot of work to have exponential gains. I can't make my life 30 percent better in a short period of time anymore, but I know when I was just starting, that happened all the time.

Another cool thing about making progress is that it becomes infectious. Underdogs get one thing going for them, and then the next thing becomes easier. It's like rolling something downhill—once you get it started, everything becomes much easier.

I've seen this so many times in my own life, and in other underdogs who came from nowhere to achieve massive success. You just have to start taking action, learning from those actions—whether you succeed or fail—and improving until you get it right.

Then, you use this momentum to rocket past the privileged and take their place. Kind of like what I did with the fishing.

REELING IT IN

We got to the first hole and nobody was catching fish. So everyone moved to the second hole. Maybe one person caught a fish. Not that any of us were saying anything, but I could tell everyone was getting a little discouraged and frustrated.

Not me. I was quietly obsessing on what was not working. I would isolate each little thing, test if it worked or not, and then confirm it. And I did something revolutionary with that knowledge:

I did less of what was not working.

Then, when I found something that was working, I did more of it.

I know right, you must be laughing your ass off right now, thinking *What the hell is he talking about, everyone does that!*

And that's where you'd be wrong.

No one else was really focusing on learning, or so it seemed. Maybe it was the fact that my grandfather, who died when I was ten, was such an inspiration and role model in my life. He loved fly fishing, and maybe deep down I wanted to make him proud. And yes, that is another underdog advantage. Passion! They seemed to be just casting away, sometimes faster and more often but without adjustments.

The first thing I noticed was that when you walked up to the stream, it was so clear. You see, trout are really smart, and they can see through the water. If they saw you coming, they'd swim away. So on one hole, I snuck up to the stream on my hands and knees. And bamm I started getting hits.

Then I realized that there is a real art to the amount of line you leave out. If you don't keep the line tight, the fish hit the fly and the slack makes it possible for them to spit the hook out. But with a tighter line, you can set the hook before they spit it out.

I started keeping the length controlled. Now I was starting to catch fish. And for those of you worriers, not one fish was harmed. All returned with love.

So I was sneaking up to holes and keeping proper line tightness. Then I realized that where I cast was key. The turbulent parts were no good, and the flats didn't work—but where the turbulence hit the flat was perfect. That's where their food was circulating. If I landed it there, every time I got a hit.

I put all of these things together by the seventh hole, and I was catching fish after fish after fish. I look over and Lewis, seeing me catch all these fish, was just casting again and again, faster and faster. He didn't give up, he kept getting back out there, but he didn't change anything.

We got to the last hole and, with my process perfected, I caught thirteen trout. That gave me twenty-two overall, and the runaway victory.

Brendon: "That's amazing man, I caught like two fish, I'm horrible."

Russell: "How the heck is that possible that you caught thirteen on the last hole, has anyone else caught thirteen all day?"

The answer was no.

Lewis: "That's my partner—champion by a mile."

Dean: "Yeah, I guess I just got lucky."

But it wasn't luck at all.

Here's the thing. Every guy there was not only a great dude, but also very successful. We all had the same rods. We had the same line with the same bait, all fishing in the same water at the same time of day for the same fish.

Isn't this the same in business? No matter what business you are in or want to explore, there are others out there with the same advantages as you. But most people will overlook the obvious, the little things that become the big things. Most people don't realize that their unfair advantages are actually the things most of the world thinks are their disadvantage.

What was the difference between us? Only one that I could see:

I obsessed on figuring out what wasn't working on the fly like I do in business every day, and did less of it or adjusted.

Then I acknowledged everything that was working and did more of it aggressively, and tweaked it until it got better and better. Again, like I have been doing in business for over thirty years BECAUSE inside I am an underdog.

In essence, I learned from my actions, and I used that knowledge to improve my future actions.

Hey, I never said the underdog advantages were complicated. They aren't. Often the simplest stuff is what makes the biggest difference, if you actually apply it.

As I write this chapter and look back over my life and fortunate success, I know I have had lots of failures. I talk about a bunch of them in this book. But I think what has kept me relevant and able to grow my income, my business, and my relationships year after year is that I've never lost sight of what an advantage it is to be underestimated.

I still incorporate this mindset into every area of my life.

Even a friendly fishing competition.

UNDERDOG CHALLENGE #3

So for this challenge, I want you to really analyze what parts of your life are not working at the level you want.

If you're in great shape, you're analyzing the results you get with the food you eat and you adjust accordingly, you're analyzing the exercise you do and you're making tweaks. That's why your body looks the way it does or you feel the way you do.

If you have a magnificent relationship, you're intuitively just making decisions all the time, based on a feedback loop. If you say certain things and it makes your spouse, your significant other upset, you adjust, you find out why they like it or don't. You're measuring and doing less of what doesn't work and you're doing more of what does.

As simple as this sounds, it's not rocket science. Most people avoid it, especially when it comes to your business and making more money. When a business is not working, people tend to just run faster. It's like you're on a treadmill with it on level six, and you want to get a mile down the road and when you're not actually moving, you put the treadmill up to 10. But you're still on a damn treadmill—you aren't actually going to get anywhere unless tired and overwhelmed is the destination you are looking for.

How many so-called entrepreneurs quit a job to create a business that takes twice their time to make half the money, but they're so-called "in business for themselves" at least, and killing themselves. It's because they're not measuring what doesn't work and adjusting and doing less of it, and observing obsessively and tracking what does work and trying to do it better.

Same with marketing and sales. The reason that you might have this book in your hands is because I obsess on marketing. I watch every metric of who watches my videos. Do people click through on my videos? If they click through, do they watch the video I created for them? Do they like the video? Do they buy the book? Do they get it shipped priority? Do they post a review? I measure every one of those, and if any section is not working I work diligently to make it better or stop doing it. If it's doing well, then I do more of it.

Open your eyes up to the things that are working in your life. You are consciously or unconsciously measuring, tweaking, and adjusting. And the areas of your life that aren't working? If you're overweight, if you're broke, if your relationship sucks, it's very obvious you are not doing those things.

Where in your life or business are you not measuring your results enough?

Whether it's your marketing, your conversations with coworkers or higher-ups, your love life, or anything else— where are you not succeeding, but also not eliminating the things that don't move the needle in your life, or are just toxic?

Where can you dumb things down a bit and start to measure?

What is it that you want to grow or get better at?

What are you doing that isn't working?

How can you stop or tweak it?

What is working?

How can you measure it better?

How can you do more of this, enhance it, or add fuel to this fire?

What is the best outcome over the next 30, 60, and 120 days?

What is the worst outcome if you leave this as it is and do nothing?

CHAPTER 4

Underdogs Are Relentlessly Resourceful

Underdogs come from big cities, small towns, wealthy families and poor ones, divorced parents and those that are together, great family lives and horrific childhoods, college degrees and not even a high school education. There is no prejudice when it comes to underdogs, and we are everywhere. When we are taught how to unlock our true potential nothing can stop us.

Jenna Kutcher grew up in a small town of 5,000. She went to school for business and thought she was going to do the corporate thing. To her, success looked like a corner office in a big building, wearing high heels and being in charge.

She realized pretty quickly in her corporate journey that she flat out hated it. She landed herself in a windowless office, working fifty-hour weeks, commuting in rush hour both ways, and she felt as if her life was being sucked away from her hour by hour.

The worst part was that she worked for the Target Corporation. Being that she was from Minnesota, that's a really big deal. Target's headquartered there, and working at that office was the idea of real success for most people in the area, including her friends and family.

She was lost and unsure what to do, so she did what lots of people do in that situation: she spent money, the little money she had, to distract herself from her work unhappiness.

Then she made a different type of purchase. She bought a $300 camera on Craigslist to take personal photos as she and her fiancé planned their wedding. She ended up taking the camera to her brother and sister-in-law's wedding in Jamaica, and it was a good thing she did: they hadn't hired a wedding photographer, so Jenna took all of their photos.

It was the first wedding she ever shot, and she did a pretty good job—especially considering that she'd only ever looked at wedding magazines before. She fell in love with photography and decided that it would be her ticket out of corporate America.

The problem? She had absolutely no idea how to start a wedding photography business. She had no money to buy equipment. No time to learn photography (she was still working full time). No friends or employees to do the work for her. She seemingly had no advantages at all going for her to even consider it. Yes, when it came to her escaping the corporate world and doing elaborate weddings all over the world for fun and profit, it was a great dream. But she was such an underdog, how the hell could that even be considered as a possibility?

Knowing she didn't have many resources, she tapped into one of the most powerful tactics used by successful underdogs throughout the centuries by becoming "resourceful" and got momentum while others scratched their heads in amazement.

She did pretty well at it. Jenna was a wedding photographer for eight years and shot over 130 weddings in that time. Not only that, she was named the #1 Wedding Photographer in Wisconsin.

That would have been a great accomplishment by itself. But Jenna did much more than get her wedding photography business off the ground.

She has now built one of the most successful and profitable wedding photography businesses, teaching others how to do the same thing she did.

And that horrible position she started in with no resources—that looked so dire and bad from the outside—is precisely how a regular girl from a small town in Minnesota made all this happen.

Even as I write this, I notice that her podcast, "Goal Getters" is one of the top business podcasts in the world. How could she do that? How did the lack of resources help her?

Because Jenna understood how to use this Underdog Advantage.

THE PRIVILEGED CAN IGNORE THEIR PROBLEMS (FOR A WHILE)

When you are privileged, you can hide the things in your life that you feel are perfect and avoid them.

That works...for a little while that is.

But there's a downside to that. Like a debt you are paying interest on, the longer you wait to pay it off, the more it costs.

And avoiding your problems always costs way more.

In computer programming, this is called "technical debt" and in business, it's called "operational debt" but the point is the same in all areas:

If you don't fix your problems now when they're small, they will be big and crippling later.

This is a major problem for the privileged. When you're on top, it's so easy to ignore issues—after all, you're privileged, how bad can anything be?

And that's why the privileged unfortunately fail when they seemingly had every advantage not to. And sometimes when it goes wrong, it's catastrophic.

But more often than not, the fact that they're expected to win is what dooms them.

There was a time in the 80s when people asked if anyone could ever beat IBM in computers.

Today, they don't even sell computers anymore.

There was a time in the 90s when everyone knew Nokia would dominate mobile phones forever.

Today, they're (basically) out of business.

There was a time in the early 2000s when AOL looked unbeatable in the internet.

They no longer exist either.

The same thing happened with Borders bookstore. Remember them?

Or even better, what about Kodak? You might be too young to remember when we used to use actual physical film to take pictures, but there was a time Kodak, the company that made most of the camera film in America, was one of the biggest companies in the US. Now? Doesn't exist.

Here's the worst part: Kodak invented the digital camera, and they ignored it, because they didn't think digital was the future.

They ignored their problems (declining film sales) because they thought it was a small thing. Now, the inventors of the digital camera don't even exist.

And we all know the story of Blockbuster. They looked completely dominant and unbeatable. They had all the stores, they had all the relationships with Hollywood, they had all the money and the press...and then this little company called Netflix came along.

Do you know why Netflix was started? It was literally started because of the biggest problem with Blockbuster: late fees.

After he got a $40 late fee for *Apollo 13*, Reed Hastings founded Netflix. Not only could Blockbuster not hide from their problems, it was their biggest problem that led directly to the competitor that put them out of business.

Here is the crazy part. Blockbuster saw Netflix coming. Did a huge market research to evaluate the impact it would have on their sales. They even had the chance to buy them, but declined stating that, "people just don't want to watch movies online."

The fact was they were too privileged, they weren't hungry like the underdog startup machine that Reed Hastings was fighting for. And that little company went past them so fast it was like they were standing still.

Everyone thinks it's great to have unlimited resources. But how did it work out for all those companies?

Not good.

JENNA'S LACK OF RESOURCES LED HER TO SUCCESS

Jenna felt like her entire career has been that of an underdog, being not just a woman, but a woman in a small town, with no experience, no resources, no money, and nobody being a cheerleader for her dreams. She realized early on she had to figure things out in a different way.

So when she looked at starting a career as a wedding photographer with zero experience, she figured out with some simple math that twenty-five weddings in one year was enough to get her out of her current job.

She also knew that there were a lot of women like her, who had good taste but couldn't afford a really expensive photographer or a nice wedding, and even though she might not have had the education of a photography degree or anything like that, she could connect with those women because she was one of them. She'd just gotten married, she knew what brides wanted and how to give it to them. She knew what most people were doing wrong, at least from the bride's perspective.

She knew the power of branding and she knew the importance of speaking to people in the way that they wanted to be spoken to, especially being that she was a recent bride herself. So she leaned on the experiences that she had planning her own wedding and understanding the things that made her confident. She also thought about the decisions and things that made her wary, and had an understanding of things she was willing to invest in and not invest in.

Jenna realized very quickly that since she had very limited resources she had to be resourceful as hell, magnify what she did have, and not let what she was lacking be an anchor of doubt that would hold her back.

She said, "I built my entire brand on saying to brides, 'I understand you,' because I did. and I think that has been the center point for my marketing ever since I began. I didn't have much, but I did have the ability to pay attention to what people need and not just what they want."

Another problem: she was living in a very small town at the time. Only 1,200 people in the town she had recently moved to and she didn't know anyone.

She had no idea where to start, so she did the only thing she knew how to do: she launched a blog and started a Facebook page and was literally sliding into the DMs of anyone she could think of who was getting engaged. She had no money, so she had to hustle and do her marketing herself.

She also did something that very few people were doing at the time: she marketed directly to women who could not afford fancy weddings.

Her thought was that it was a totally underserved market. And that's where she started—so she was marketing to people at her level.

She very acutely remembered what it was like to be poor out of college, with student loans, planning a wedding. When she planned her wedding, the whole thing cost $13,000 for 200 people. She had pizza at her wedding, and her wedding dress cost $358.

So when she was marketing, she was marketing to herself and what was important to her.

She felt that targeting those at the lower end of the market took all the pressure off of her. She was able to show up and do the best she could without feeling like she was over promising and under delivering. She was slowly building her confidence, and developing her skills. When she'd show up to these jobs, she was speaking to more than just the direct clients. She would do a lot of different things for her brides.

She would even tell them that "I'll be like the fourth bridesmaid on your wedding day without any of the hassle." She let them know, "I will go run and fetch your shoes and I'll help your grandma up when she needs to stand up in church, and I'll be there with your bouquet and I'll bring extra hairspray in my bag." And then she did it.

She was anticipating what people needed before they could even ask for it. A lot of her weddings were lower budget, and they didn't have a wedding planner. For some of them, nobody had ever done a wedding before. But Jenna had been to hundreds of weddings and so she was the one that was running the show and keeping everyone calm.

And as a result of this approach—of being whatever the

bride and the family needed—she would serve their families, their teams, and whoever else was there.

Because of this "disadvantaged" approach, she never had to put a single penny into advertising. It all came from word of mouth from people that met her while she was doing her job.

What she thought was a disadvantage turned out to be her biggest advantage. Many people look at price as the differentiator, so a lot of entrepreneurs have the problem of people price shopping them. They get so upset, because they see people going for a cheaper option, but if you start as that cheaper option and you really over deliver, you can incrementally raise your prices...and that's exactly what Jenna did.

For her first twenty-five weddings, Jenna charged $2,500. By the end, she was shooting $10,000 weddings.

In our lives, we are met with obstacles and problems on a regular basis. So why is it that one person finds success and another finds excuses? It could be our upbringing, movies we watched, parents who thought they were protecting us, or a million other reasons. But what if today, at this very moment, you decided to change your perspective on the so-called obstacles you have and to make them advantages no one else could see but you?

What if you decided to just be massively resourceful in every area of you your life that you crave another level.

This resourcefulness launched Jenna into a thriving business. And at first, building her own business was really fun. But it didn't stay that way.

The worst part of success for Jenna was realizing that she'd climbed a ladder into another place where she wasn't super happy, and was trading her time for money in a way that didn't suit her. She was planning her life around other people's weddings.

That was when she and her husband decided that they wanted to try and start their family and they had to be really scheduled in that decision, because she had all of her summers booked out for weddings.

This stress may have played a part in two miscarriages, two years in a row, and she had to keep waiting to even try to grow her family just because work was coming first.

That was when she realized that she didn't want to keep doing the wedding grind. It was an amazing career, but when she had her second miscarriage during a wedding shoot, she knew it was time to make a change.

She had everything she thought she wanted, but inside she was sad, and had no idea what to do.

UNDERDOGS GET TO FACE THE TRUTH AND USE IT TO IMPROVE

This is one of the underdog advantages that I really spend a lot of time focusing on. Honestly, it's the main one that I worry about losing as I get successful:

Underdogs have to face the truth, and not hide from their problems, and this is what helps them succeed.

It is such a blessing to not be able to hide from your problems. The day that I start hiding from my problems is the last true day of success I will ever have. I try very hard to maintain a focus on issues that I deep down want to avoid, so that I can identify and then fix them. Hiding from my problems has done nothing but bring me sorrow.

By facing the truth and not hiding from their problems, underdogs gain so many advantages:

- Underdogs get to be relentlessly resourceful

- Underdogs can learn freely, without having to adhere to any dogma

- Underdogs can see clearly who they do not want to be

- Underdogs can decide who they want to become

- Underdogs can focus on progress over perfection

To put it plainly—underdogs have skin in the game, and that forces them to learn and make the best decisions possible.

Rachel Hollis knows all about having to face the truth.

When Rachel Hollis was first dating her husband Dave, there was a time when he treated her like shit. He told her, "You're not really my girlfriend." He said, "I don't tell everybody we're serious. It was just a fling."

It was pretty terrible.

Before you start to get mad at him, realize the thing that Rachel had to realize: *she allowed him to treat her that way.*

Rachel had to face the truth of this. The truth of how she let him do this to her. And she did.

So she stopped. She drew a line in the sand. She spoke her heart to him, and she said, this is not OK.

She found love within herself, set the boundaries that he had to respect it if he wanted her in his life...and lo and behold, he did.

Now they are married, have four gorgeous children, and have an amazing relationship.

I am grateful to call them friends and have spent quality time with them. They are not just great in the public's eye.

They have a solid foundation, mutual respect, and complement each other in a truly magical way.

Rachel facing her problems not only turned a not-so-great relationship into a magical one. It was the premise of her career as a writer, influencer, and businessperson that has made her a household name and the voice of millions of women around the world. If you don't know her and Dave, I encourage you to seek them out.

To get there, she had to face a hard truth about herself, and then admit that this was a problem and solve it.

To me, that's the coolest thing about being an underdog: by facing your truth, you learn faster, deeper, and it sticks. You can actually see the truth.

When you are privileged, no one tells you the truth. You are surrounded by people who make their living off telling you what it is you want to hear. They don't care about reality, they only care about how well they are pleasing you, because you are the golden goose that is feeding them.

But as an underdog, you have to face the facts, and when you do, then you can learn and grow faster than anyone around you. And it also allows you to be relentlessly resourceful as you do it.

This happened to me with Motor Millions (my first ever

information product). Once I got it on TV, and doing well in terms of sales, I still didn't have a lot of money to spend on it, because I was so in debt from how long it took to get it moving.

So instead of hiring people who were "experts" at this, I created every department myself. I created the customer service department, I created the sales department, the shipping department. I had to do the work at first for all of these divisions, set up the processes, and then hire people to do them.

Yeah, it sucked at first. This was a painful problem while I was in the thick of it.

But because I did that, I was able to make sure I got them right, and I knew exactly how each one should work because I built them. That resourcefulness helped me so much later on.

Underdogs also can use their problems to clearly see who they do, and do not, want to be.

For me, I've never wanted to be the guy "that used to be successful." The prospect of that has always made me face my painful truths and dig into my problems, because if I don't, then I'll be that guy.

But what about the true underdog. The everyday person,

probably a lot like you, who has a dream for another level of life, income, freedom, and happiness. And when life goes sideways, or the partner cheated, the company closes, the loan falls through, people don't believe in you and you go home to face a bit of desperation alone in your thoughts. And in many cases that home isn't your idea of perfection.

That person I'm describing, maybe you, has the same level of anxiety I do when I face issues in my life. But in many cases you don't have the resources (neither did I for the majority of my life) to help you see a better, faster way. You may still have to go to that job you hate, the home you despise, or the partner who isn't supportive. You don't have access to Tony Robbins, Dr. Daniel Amen, and the amazing connections and unlimited resources I've been blessed to acquire in more recent years. And I realize that now more than ever, and that is the main reason for writing this book.

Going through my divorce really helped get me back to that resourcefulness mindset, and gave me so much compassion for the people that I want to serve. I used to be that person, that underdog who didn't feel like I had help or a voice, and I kinda lost some connection with that version of me because of my success.

Basically, my divorce brought me back and even deeper than ever before. It was the hardest thing I'd ever faced. Jonelle, my former wife, and I knew the relationship was over for many years, but my turbulent childhood came racing back to me in my late 40s and I projected all those horrible memories on to what my kids would experience once the divorce was final. I felt the pain of not having them every day at my core and it created this empty place in my heart. I predicted all these terrible things that would happen with my kids and it caused deep sadness, uncontrollable anxiety, and a darkness I'd never experienced.

It was so scary because I wasn't facing it. I was just focusing on what could go wrong. Then finally I stopped being paralyzed and ignoring the pain, and starting being resourceful. As I had done in business so many times prior, being an underdog, I steered into the problem, faced it head-on, and realized more than ever that my next level of life, happiness, parenting, peace, and love lived on the other side of my biggest fear. The day I remembered that powerful underdog advantage of being relentlessly resourceful and facing my problems was the day I snapped back to the Dean I used to be. The day everything started to shift. The day my life started to climb to a whole new peak.

My confidence helped drive an elegant and peaceful divorce. My ex and I are truly better friends now than ever before. My kids are happier, yes, happy because they see their parents at peace and thriving. And through that journey I discovered more of my own flaws, what I did wrong, how I could improve, and made a decision on who I would become for the rest of my life.

On the other side of facing my biggest fears, I met Lisa, the love of my life, and was a better man because of all the crap I went through and discovered by facing the shit storm. As I finish this book, we just got married and I'm experiencing a love that I didn't even know existed. My kids adore her and they are truly connected. My ex and my wife are friends too. Crazy, I know. But this is what underdogs can create in their lives by being resourceful and facing their own shit storms with a new focus.

My divorce did more than just make me grow as a man, father, leader, and new husband—it made me realize that resourcefulness got me here and allowed me to grow through this experience. It inspired me to push harder, write this book, create more tools, and do all I can to inspire you to your greatness. To be that voice I wish I had when I was an underdog and felt like I was all alone with no help and no roadmap. You are meant for more, you can achieve it, and I hope to be that spark to ignite your true destiny.

Now, I'm not endorsing divorce. Do all you can to fix your relationship, use your underdog advantages to empower what you have and look for your own flaws before pointing fingers. But for us it was the right decision.

My divorce taught me something: it's easy to see the light when you're in the dark. You can't see the stars in the day. You can only see them at the darkest part of the night, right?

Same thing goes in all areas of life when you're an underdog, and all your problems are right there, visible because it is dark in some areas of your life. Don't look away, face them and realize your next level lives on the other side of them.

Clearly seeing your problems and addressing them explodes your progress, instead of worrying about perfection and being stuck.

As crazy as this sounds, at the age of fifty as I write this book, I realize one thing to be a matter of fact: "The bigger the problems you choose to face, the bigger the success that lives on the other side of them."

You should be excited about that, it's a massive underdog advantage.

JENNA'S FIRST SUCCESS CAUSED HER TO FAIL...AND THEN LED TO SUCCESS AGAIN

Jenna hired a business coach. He encouraged her to start teaching, because he noticed that she was really good at branding and marketing, and she'd been able to grow and scale this six-figure photography business in just a few years. Very few wedding photographers could do that in any amount of time.

At first, Jenna was resistant. Who was she to coach other wedding photographers?

Her business coach pointed out the obvious: "How many photographers are as successful as you? And how many who are successful started where you did, with no money, no time, doing this as a side hustle, no photography background even? That makes you the most qualified to teach it."

That was the thing Jenna was missing: the disadvantages she had starting off were actually what laid the foundation for her exponential success. Plainly put, it was why she's so well-equipped to teach this to other people.

She realized that she used to look down on herself for having to hustle and improvise so much to overcome her obstacles, but those are the people that are really making it happen, because they're forced to.

Even though time and money were her two biggest pitfalls at the time, that made her super scrappy, and it helped her to understand some essential truths in business.

For example, she realized she didn't always have to pay other people to do things. Sometimes you are better off doing things yourself and learning them. She learned how to code a website and she learned how to market. She learned that sometimes marketing and sales was nothing more than reaching out and connecting with people one on one, instead of waiting for them to come to you.

When she thought back to those days that she was so mad because she couldn't go out and buy a brand new camera and a bunch of lenses and all this—she realized this was also a huge benefit. Not having a great camera meant she had to really understand photography, and understand how to get people to do the things that would give them the best pictures, because the camera wouldn't do it for her.

She learned so much about photography; for example she could look at a photo and realize what the photographer said or how they directed it. This allowed her to approach brides in a very different way, and do the things that made them feel valued. She learned to actually listen to them, to make them feel important.

She started with the lower end of the market because she had no other option at the time. But this was an advantage as well. She realized that when most people reach out about something, they'll ask how much you charge. She saw that this approach meant starting off a relationship with money first.

So instead, when she did sales, she would ask about the bride first. Tell me about you. What are you passionate about? What are you excited about?

This helped her close so many clients, even when she wasn't the cheapest option anymore. And even better, it was market research. The more she listened to her potential clients, the more she understood what they were interested in. This allowed her to message things right, and to make them feel valued beyond just the dollar value.

This also told her exactly what she needed to do in order to under promise and over deliver—because that's how word of mouth happens. That's how you gain people's trust and grow your clientele slowly. Her whole business was built this way, and the lightbulb went on and she realized she could teach this.

She learned to tailor the experience of her client, and that she wanted to offer services based on her experiences as a bride and the time she spent with her clients.

Yeah, just about anyone can go pick up a camera and take photos and deliver that. But Jenna had learned that not everyone can give an experience like that, and that is what made her become the best wedding photographer.

She said it best, "I don't think I was a true artist. I think I was incredible at serving people well. And I could teach that to people. Anyone can be nice, listen, and serve."

She was skilled at all of this precisely because she had to be so relentlessly resourceful when she started as a true underdog.

Today, Jenna has a multimillion-dollar business that is all online. It gives her the freedom to work from anywhere. When I talked to her for this book, she was at her own vacation home in Hawaii with her family for the month.

She also teaches courses to female entrepreneurs now. She runs one of the top business podcasts in the world, and she does it all from anywhere she wants and on her own terms.

All because she had to face her problems and be relentlessly resourceful in solving them.

UNDERDOG CHALLENGE #4

I spent a lot of time in this chapter allowing you to see through the lens of Jenna Kutcher. Maybe a part of you can resonate with this incredible young woman, who just decided one day that she was enough, and she had enough.

All the disadvantages she had could have held her back,

should have kept her exactly where she was, where she was unhappy, but safe. But she used those same things to actually help move her forward.

In this underdog challenge, I would love for you to do two things:

1. Identify what is the biggest fear in your life and how you can face it.

2. And then stop looking or hoping for more resources in your life and rather identify places where you can become more resourceful with what you already have.

Stop looking away; how can you face it head-on? Is it easy? Hell no. But life's going to be difficult either way.

Why not power through the problems so you can realize what so many of us have?

Your next level of life truly does live on the other side of the thing you fear the most.

Where in your life have you admitted defeat? Where you thought the odds were stacked against you so much that you should stay put. Where you have made the decision to stay in that corner office that Jenna was once in with no windows, thinking it was successful because it's what you once imagined.

Success comes from resourcefulness at its core. From George Washington to Jenna Kutcher, and every successful underdog in between, they all found a way to use resourcefulness above all else.

So, with such a beautiful example in black and white from this young lady who started with the cards stacked against her, and ended up fulfilling her every dream, write down the problem you are finally going to face and decide at this very moment how you can become ten times more resourceful. No matter where the starting point is for you, it's time you have your own story worthy of telling the world.

CHAPTER 5

Underdogs Self-Educate

"Dean, this isn't going to work. It's time to shut it down."

I can't tell you how many times I've heard that in my life.

But this time was different. I was losing a lot of money at warp speed, with no end in sight.

The worst part: I truly had no idea what the hell I was doing.

And I had no master plan for how to fix the problem, so it seemed inevitable that I was heading for a major crash.

I was totally out of ideas.

You see, I was done creating my first information product on how to profit from flipping used cars (the same strategy

I used to make money right out of high school) and the way I decided to sell it was through an infomercial.

I used every dollar I had saved, plus I maxed out credit cards and borrowed some money as well to produce my first infomercial.

I was trying every possible option to make this work, but to be honest, I was floundering badly. I didn't know what I didn't know and faking it until you make it wasn't working anymore.

The only thing I was sure about was that I was losing a lot of money. To the tune of about $5,000 a week going out the door. Which at the time was a huge amount of money to me.

I was stressing big time. My family tried to get me to quit, and the truth is, for the first time ever I almost took them up on it.

But you know, there's one big difference between my successes and my failures: when I was successful, it's because I didn't try to do everything myself, but instead found people to help me. When I sought out experts to teach me the things I didn't know, and took my education into my own hands, things exponentially got better.

So I stopped feeling sorry for myself, and I started looking for who could help me.

PRIVILEGED PEOPLE TEND TO ACT LIKE THEY KNOW EVERYTHING

When you're privileged, it's really hard to show weakness. To not look like you have everything under control is to invite criticism and opponents.

Instead, you have to pretend like you have a handle on all of it. No matter how bad things get, you are always "crushing it." If you're barely struggling to make payroll, doesn't matter, if you are privileged, you have to be "growing like crazy." No matter what the reality is behind the scenes, you have to pretend it's great.

If you don't, then people think you are weak. They could look down on you. They stop wanting to do business with you or be associated with you. If they see even a hint of failure around you, most people move on to the up and comer. No one wants to be associated with someone on the way down—especially if you are already established.

Because of this, the privileged often have a hard time asking for help. They create a persona of always having everything under control. Asking for help is, in the minds of many successful people, a sign of weakness.

This makes it really hard to admit they need help, and then go find the help they need. Which is unfortunate, because in so many instances that I have personally witnessed, they usually have the epiphany to ask for assistance once it's too late.

Those already in power are also very constrained in what ideas they can use. They have to only work with the "right" people and do the "right" things. They can't find the best individual if that person would look bad to work with because of lack of experience, credentials, or status amongst peers. In many instances they have to keep up appearances. They have to do what everyone else is doing and can only consider the options that other people say are safe.

In most cases underdogs (or those that think like an underdog) don't have that privilege, could care less, and will utilize whomever they can to help them reach their goals.

"HEY, I HAVE A STORY TOO."

"You're paying $200 dollars for a bunch of tapes of this guy talking? Wow, you finally lost your mind. When you're done buying that I have a bridge I want to sell you. Heck I'll talk to you right now for free!"

One of my closest friends at the time pretty much said those exact words when I told him how excited I was to receive the course I bought off of an infomercial from this guy named Tony Robbins.

I had never bought anything like that before. At the time I didn't even read books. So this was a stretch for even me.

But when I watched him talk, it spoke directly into my heart. I remember thinking, "He's talking to me." For some reason I trusted him. I just felt he had a better path to follow than the one I was on.

His course made such a huge impact on my life. I'd never been exposed to anything like this; I didn't even know what personal growth and personal development was, and all of a sudden I started realizing all these new things about myself. It was Tony Robbins who taught me self-awareness.

"Oh, I should be focusing on the solution, not the problem."

"Oh, I'm angry, stressed, or envious because I never practice gratitude."

"Huh, that's interesting—what DOES it mean if life happens for me and not to me?"

This and hundreds of other little things may seem obvious to you right now, but to me at the time, each of these were groundbreaking moments in my life.

I listened to those tapes over and over and over.

Yes cassette tapes, that's how long ago it was.

And because of Tony's Power Talk series (interviews with people he respected), I then found Wayne Dyer, Eckart Tolle, Deepak Chopra, Coach John Wooden, and many others that I went deep on as well. And from there I started to notice other infomercials and people like Carlton Sheets and Don Lapre sharing their knowledge on TV to help others go faster while they made money. The more I watched, the more I learned, the more I wanted in.

I bought their courses as well to see how they laid them out and learn whatever I could. I was being exposed to self-education and also learning what direct response marketing was. The more I dug in, the more obsessed I got. I could help people go faster in life and get paid to do it. Holy crap, this is an industry!

I started to realize just how many people must have been buying for them to be running all of these commercials, and I was hooked.

Then it hit me: I have a good story. I have something to teach people as well.

Just seven years ago I was working at a shitty garage with my dad, and now I'm a millionaire making great money. I went from a 300-square-foot apartment to building and living in one of the most expensive homes in my town. And I have not one, but two companies that are doing great.

I started trying to write my own course. I set my alarm for 5:00 a.m. every day, and wrote each morning for two hours.

It was horrible at first. That's why I said I was "trying."

But after lots of thrown away pages, I ended up with a course I called "Motor Millions," which was a step-by-step process on how to make money with used cars just like I had done in my hometown.

At the end, I was pretty proud of it too. I tested it on some friends, they understood it, implemented it, and best of all, had crazy good results. I named all the sections and designed the graphics for the four manuals, and designed the two CD and one DVD covers.

The course was done, it looked great, and the information was solid. Now I had to sell it. And why not an infomercial like Tony Robbins did? It got me to buy and impacted my life in a huge way, so why not?

I started recording infomercials I saw on TV and watching them obsessively. Like, I could not stop watching. Every cut, every camera angle, everything I could see, or at least tried to see.

So with a course in hand, it was time to create the way to sell it. I laid out all the bullets, scripting, the flow, and the theme of my first infomercial.

Still waking up at 5 a.m., I probably spent another month or so getting prepared, writing, and tweaking the script. I obsessed on this. I drew out storyboards, pasted them on my wall; I went all-in on creating my first infomercial.

Then I hired a production crew to film this thirty-minute commercial using most all my money and a bunch of borrowed cash. After going back and forth for about four weeks we were ready, and they arrived at my home to film day one.

I thought I would film in the front yard of my home, because by my standards back then it was a freaking mansion and I was damn proud of it.

I had no idea all the stuff a camera crew brings to film a TV shoot. A truck just for the lights, a whole truck just for a huge dolly that went on tracks like a small train, another truck for electrical and audio, and so many people. I remember thinking, "No wonder it cost a small fortune!"

They spent at least three hours setting everything up, got

the cameras rolling, and the director points at me and says, "Let's do this!"

To be honest, by then I was a little overwhelmed by it all. And of course nervous as hell. That inner voice questioning every single part of this was not so silent anymore. I'm guessing you know that dialogue with yourself when stepping off the path of what's normal. That one that says "You're nuts," or "You don't know what you are doing" or "You are going to lose all your money" those thoughts were all playing on repeat in my mind.

But I practiced what personal growth hacks I had at the time and got myself in a better place and I was ready to "do this."

I mean I'd been working on cars and making money with them for ten years by then. So I can do this, right? Talking on camera about it will be no different than when I was teaching friends. Right?

So I step in front of the camera, the director rolls his finger in a circular motion to the camera guy, I opened my mouth to speak, and nothing came out.

I mean nothing.

Pure cottonmouth.

I paused, said excuse me, drank a bunch of water, but then

I started sweating terribly. I got in front of the camera to start again, but the director told me to change my shirt. It was soaked through with sweat.

I finally got back out there, and then I couldn't remember one thing to say.

I was a complete nervous wreck.

Then I started getting mad at myself.

So I did what most consciously evolved humans would do. I mediated, aligned my thoughts and my energy and...

I'm lying. I didn't do any of that shit. I had zero skills like that back then. I went into my kitchen, found some tequila leftover from a party that summer and did a shot.

That shot relaxed me, the cottonmouth went away, all my thoughts on what to say came racing back to me and the shoot went great.

I'm lying again. The tequila gave me a buzz, the cottonmouth got worse, and the few words I did remember were now totally gone.

So after several attempts, I realized it was pointless. I called day one a wrap and sent the production team home. It was a total disaster.

That night as I sat alone in my house, full of shame, I did not for one second feel like I had any Underdog Advantages. I felt like a piece of crap loser who wasted his money, who couldn't deliver when he needed to, and that the world was going to laugh at me for trying.

And yes, that's all true with no exaggeration.

UNDERDOGS CAN ADMIT THEY DON'T KNOW THINGS AND SEARCH FOR THE HELP THEY NEED

When I was in high school, my guidance counselor sat me down after she saw I didn't take my SATs. I didn't see any reason to take it and fail it and look like an idiot when I wasn't even considering going to college.

She said, "Oh, no SAT? Okay. So you could work in the local factory. Or I guess fix cars with your dad. Those are your options, you idiot."

Ok she didn't say the "you idiot" part, but the way she said the rest, she may as well have.

There was only one factory in my little town in upstate New York town called Triple R Industries. They were hiring people at five dollars an hour back then. And continuing to work with my dad at his collision repair shop was cool, but it wasn't making much money at the time.

It seemed as if she was saying the choice was: go to college like your friends and have a wonderful life versus going to work in a factory, or being a grease monkey, and be a loser. There was nothing in the middle to her.

And that is the way such a huge majority of people around the world think. They can't even conceive of other paths to success in life, or other ways to learn.

But not *everyone* sees it this way.

You know who disagrees with my high school guidance counselor? Ginni Rometty, the CEO of IBM. She said, "Forget blue-collar, forget white-collar. This is the world of new-collar, and new-collar people are those who seek specialized knowledge through self-education."

They're the ones she wants to hire. They're the ones that immediately go to work. They're the ones who solve problems and get stuff done.

I would say the most common underdog advantage I see in most every wildly successful self-made person I've met is they invest in self-education, and they ask for help from others who have already accomplished what they are looking to achieve.

Whether that's a book, a mentor, a mastermind, a coaching group, or a community, successful underdogs know the fastest way to the next level and to break through barriers is to learn from others already playing the game at a higher level.

Whether they went to college or not, it doesn't matter, underdogs who accomplish astronomical feats took the road less traveled and learned from others' trial and error.

The world is realizing what successful underdogs have known for centuries and gobbling up self-education at a staggering rate. Right now, as I write this book, there's 335 million dollars a day spent on non-traditional education. And even crazier, Forbes says that's heading to a billion dollars a day by 2025. It's literally one of the fastest-growing industries in the world.

For me, it started with Tony Robbins taking my money for information. And through him I learned about so many other people who've been my guiding path to my full potential. Now at this phase of my life I get to help others reach their goals faster and easier by providing them a roadmap based on my years of experience.

Hopefully this book alone provides you at least one thing that helps you on your journey. And if so, then welcome to the wonderful world of self-education and discovering what Henry Ford, Andrew Carnegie, Bill Gates, Arianna Huffington, Richard Branson, and so many of the world's most successful people throughout time quietly discovered as their biggest underdog advantage.

Napoleon Hill, in 1937, wrote this in *Think and Grow Rich*:

> Successful men, in all callings, never stop acquiring specialized knowledge related to their major purpose, business, or profession. Those who are not successful usually make the mistake of believing that the knowledge acquiring period ends when one finishes school. The truth is that schooling does but little more than to put one in the way of learning how to acquire practical knowledge.

And it was gaining specialized knowledge from others who had already had success in the world that I desired that made me realize that my guidance counselor, and most of the world, had it wrong.

Gaining specialized knowledge is the best-kept secret to blowing by the competition, surprising the family who doubted you, and reaching that level of abundance you deserve.

And what does specialized knowledge on steroids look like? Masterminds, Groups, and Workshops.

You see, before the books, before even Tony Robbins, before I was successful in the eyes of the world—I was just an underdog trying to change my destiny. Trying to run away from a life I didn't like.

But looking back, I was lucky enough to realize that learning from traditional education didn't work for me, and learning from my own trial and error had a huge cost in time and energy.

I learned to seek out assistance from others who had experience or mastered what I was seeking to achieve. In my early twenties, I had three dear friends that were all over sixty, and one in his eighties, who all helped me figure out some of the basics of real estate and business.

But it wasn't until I realized there was a next level to learning from others' experiences through immersing myself with groups of like-minded people all desiring a similar outcome that things really improved.

To share obstacles and have others who have already been through them show you the fast lane to solve them and avoid complications. To reveal opportunities in front of you and have a group or individual show you the blueprint they used to accomplish what you desire.

It was about fifteen years ago when I joined my first mastermind, and by lunchtime I remember thinking, "Why doesn't the world know about this?" In that first mastermind, I can track about a million dollars in additional revenue that year alone.

And since then I have attended at least 300 days of masterminds and spent over a million dollars attending them or hosting them. There is zero doubt that it has been my ultimate underdog advantage to grow my life, my income, and my success year after year.

I know what you are thinking: a million of dollars on masterminds? That's crazy!

Granted, that might seem a little extreme—but is it, really?

My companies and my brands have done, collectively, over 1 billion dollars in sales of products and services, and I can equate the most growth, the biggest breakthroughs, and solving the biggest problems from attending those masterminds.

That million dollars and the 300+ days were actually the best investment of my life.

See, that's the big thing that masterminds taught me: the more I can learn, the faster I can learn, the more people I can learn from, the better I am going to do.

All I had to do was be humble and ask for help, then implement it. It was amazing!

And learning from others does not mean you must find life-long sages or people who know everything. Sometimes you simply want to learn from the person who is one chapter ahead of you.

Let me explain. If you wanted to gain some unfair advantages when it comes to sales, how beneficial would it be if you found someone in the same sales process as you, yet they've been in the game one year longer than you. If you were able to spend a weekend with them, how much information could you learn from their failures and their successes to go faster? A lot, right? What would that be worth?

If somebody was marketing on YouTube a year longer than you, doing real estate a year longer than you, cutting hair, fly fishing, understanding wine, or a million other things, how much faster could you go if you could start off from where they are now?

Let me give you just a few real-life examples of how what I learned in masterminds changed my life.

I was at in a mastermind in Toronto with my friend Dean Jackson. During the event he shared with me a stealth-like email process he called the nine-word email (you can google it, start some self-education right there). He shared it with me so I would use it and that's exactly what I did.

I sent it out in less than a week and completely filled a

$10,000 per person, one-day mastermind. This one strategy allowed me to get a killer group of people ready to learn my strategies to scale their businesses. And this damn email did the job with no salesperson, no complexity—just happy clients. And it really is just a simple email that asks a question to people who have expressed interest in it before. That's it. So simple, but so effective.

And it continues to this day. While at a mastermind in Puerto Rico very recently, Jenna Kutcher, who you learned about earlier, taught me that I wasn't paying enough attention to my female fans, "I don't know if you realize it, but you have a huge amount of us loving your stuff but much of what you do, mostly the look, is very masculine. All the edges are sharp, colors very harsh." So we started softening a few things and we watched an exponential change in the way women post on my Instagram account.

And then when Tony Robbins and I launched the "Knowledge Business Blueprint" course, 60 percent of the buyers were women. And that was just one little shift that she helped me see.

When I was going through a divorce, I worked with the greatest love coach on the planet, Annie Lala, to help me understand love in a way I never did before. She helped me with the anxiety of being separated from my kids, while simultaneously teaching me what real love looked like.

So we were able to exit a relationship with compassion, my kids are thriving and my former wife and I are good friends.

I also discovered a better version of me and knew exactly what to do when looking for the next relationship in my life. I learned what love really meant, including love of self. I was able to take her ten years of obsessing on what true love means, how to live as a pure person, and I was able to adopt that in my life in months because of self-education. The end result is I've become a better human, I understand connection on another level, and I'm now married to the love of my life.

That's just a few of hundreds, maybe thousands, of break-throughs I got from self-education. I could write an entire book of simple yet powerful things I learned from master-minds that allowed me to avoid complexity and stress and go faster toward greater success, impact, and wealth.

I mean look at it this way. What is a skill, expertise, hobby, or passion that you have, that took you a few years or a decade or more to get good at? Think of all the failures and wins along the way. Now let me ask you this. If your current self could run into the version of you when you were first starting, how much would it be worth for the older you to spend a weekend teaching the younger you how to avoid the potholes and how to add fuel to the wins?

142 · THE UNDERDOG ADVANTAGE

Priceless.

That's why people pay so much for high-quality masterminds, groups, and workshops.

The really big thing here is the mindset around this type of
learning. When I was an underdog, I didn't have this mindset (until Motor Millions) and it really held me back. Now, I
don't pretend I know everything. I don't act like it. I admit
I know nothing, and then I actively seek as much help as I
can from people who have already been there.

See, what most people don't understand is that this is SUCH
a huge advantage.

I want you to understand this, it's so important. Most of the
world just follow the norms. Most people are restricted by
the idea of general knowledge that they learned in school.
They're held back, they're handcuffed. They think that they
have to learn the way you are taught through traditional
education. They go to school, they imitate the privileged,
they never have to be or try to be resourceful, they just cut
the check for the best college they can get into and that's
it. But they're all missing the thing that underdogs figured
out a long time ago: **self-education.**

We live in a new world. You have access to training like
never before. Even in my youth, in the eighties and nineties
that wasn't available. Now it's everywhere. So it's all about

finding somebody who's doing what you want to do. Even if they're one chapter ahead of you, but they're doing it better, bigger, stronger than you; learn from them.

They have experience; extract their knowledge, whether that's a mentor, whether that's a group, a mastermind, a book, a course, or a workshop. Underdogs find unfair advantages through self-education.

Underdogs don't follow the same path everyone else does. They craft their own road map and are rewarded greatly for it. Being an underdog gives you a huge advantage: you are forced to learn things on your own, and see things no one else is seeing, and develop the skills and traits that others aren't, because they are just doing what everyone else is doing.

I was forced to learn this, but once I got it, it became an obsession. It's because I wasn't privileged. I didn't have the advantage of a top school, or parents that were savvy to business, or a relative that was wealthy that told me how to manage my money.

That's why Tony Robbins and I decided to expose "Self-Education" on a whole new level. What started as a mission for us has now become a movement. Tens of thousands of people are already using our blueprint to extract what they know—a skill, a hobby, a passion—and share it with the world to make impact and profits.

Our goal and mission is to make Self-Education the new norm. Because if we didn't have it in our lives, who knows where we would be.

We want to make it so that if you die someday with knowledge in your head and you don't share it with those who need it, you should feel guilty.

We know how important this is, and we desperately want to help other people do this as well, and utilize the most important underdog advantage: self-education.

If you would like to learn how you could make an impact on the world and get paid to do it at the same time by tapping into the $355 million dollar-per-day knowledge industry, then go to kbbsecret.com and register to watch a special two-hour training where Tony and I pull back the curtain on our sixty years of combined time in this industry.

The training is phenomenal, and it will open your eyes up to a whole new world of opportunity, growth, impact, and new revenue. Go register and pick a time that best fits your schedule and see for yourself why the world is talking about the Knowledge Business Blueprint.

MOTOR MILLIONS BECOMES A HIT

I honestly just thought I was gonna get on camera and talk seamlessly with no problem.

Was I wrong.

Even though the first day was a total loss, I didn't quit. I had them come back the next day, and I was ready then.

Yeah, I kinda sucked, and it took forever to get the shots right, but I was able to actually say the script I wrote and get the commercial in the can.

On the last day, the director basically handed me the footage. And after ninety seconds of "hell yeah" celebrating, reality sunk in and I thought to myself, what the hell do I do now?

He recommended I hire an editor out of Poughkeepsie, NY. So I did. I sat down with Ralph (the editor), and we edited frame by frame, imitating what I saw through so many other shows I had watched obsessively on TV. I'd literally look at another infomercial, get an idea then edit mine, look at another, edit that, look at how they did the call to action, hit pause on theirs and edit mine. I had no idea what I was doing other than modeling what was already working with my own twist.

---

146 · THE UNDERDOG ADVANTAGE

Eventually, we got done with the infomercial. But I realized...I had no clue what to do next.

Seriously, what do you do with an infomercial? How do you get it on TV? Yes I was that naive.

I was stumped.

So I started calling TV stations. Most of them laughed at me or thought I was an idiot. I got nowhere.

After about two months of trying, I was legit depressed. I had my infomercial on exactly ZERO channels.

Then I got a break.

Don Lapre, one of the guys who I mentioned earlier who had an infomercial on what seemed like every station, at every hour of the day, went out of business. He had hundreds of people working for him, and they all lost their jobs overnight. He was based in Phoenix, so I flew out there and started meeting people who used to work with him. I eventually got connected to his media manager, Sandy. She was the one who used to book all his commercials. She was a wealth of knowledge. Like, more than I could have ever imagined you needed to know.

I didn't realize it then, but I was once again using the powerful underdog advantage of being resourceful and learning from someone who has already been there. I didn't pretend to her that I knew what I was doing. I was completely transparent and she was up for the challenge of teaching me and then working together.

I hired her and she came in with the Rolodex and went to work. She knew exactly who to call to book the media. She set me up with the company that takes the inbound phone calls. She helped me find script templates. She filled in, like, ten years of work in a few months. I could not have done this without her.

So for the next year, I lived back and forth between New York and Arizona. I'd go to Marlboro, my little town, and literally work on cars, go to car auctions, flip houses, and do my normal business. Then, I'd take that money, fly back to Phoenix, and use it all up trying to get my knowledge business working.

I wish I could tell you that things just worked out easily.

That would be a lie.

For a long time that year, I was losing about five grand a week on the infomercial. I had to hustle on my New York businesses to cover this loss. Not an easy task, in fact it was so damn stressful.

That was another time where I questioned myself.

I really asked myself—what the hell am I doing? I had these profits in my New York companies, why wasn't I happy with that? Why wasn't I satisfied? I owned real estate, I owned a good collision shop and sold used cars.

I doubted myself. I really did.

And I almost quit.

But I didn't. I thought about how Tony took my money and helped my life. I wanted to do that, and I wasn't going out without a much bigger fight.

So I kept pushing, and I kept tracking down everyone who knew something that could help me, and I worked with them. I eventually joined masterminds and just kept flooding my mind with specialized knowledge specifically in the direct response marketing industry.

And eventually Motor Millions broke out and became a hit. But stronger than that, it was the launching pad for everything I've done in the self-education industry. From twenty years on TV nonstop, multiple *New York Times* best-selling books, meeting and partnering with my heroes, speaking on stages with 15,000 people or more, impacting millions of lives all the way to writing this very sentence to you.

And none of this would have happened if I hadn't discovered the underdog advantage of self-education and learning from others who have already been there.

UNDERDOG CHALLENGE #5

In this chapter, I hope I exposed what I believe to be my ultimate unfair advantage, my ultimate underdog advantage. And that's self-education.

And I didn't know it was a fancy term, like self-education, at the time when I started acquiring knowledge from people outside of the traditional school system. But now that this is my life, now that it's made such an impact, I wanted this chapter to virtually grab you by the shoulders and shake you and make sure you're not stuck in what the world has programmed into our brains, that there's only one path to learning, there's only one model, and that's traditional education. As Napoleon Hill said in 1937, "Successful people, in all callings, never stop acquiring specialized knowledge related to their major purpose, business, or profession."

And with the world evolving, and seeing that self-education is the way to their full potential.

And what a great time to be alive with self-education truly becoming the new norm. Over the next ten years, I see employees and employers being more apt to hire based on their specialized knowledge and not their traditional schooling. In my own organization, I hire based on values and specialized knowledge. I could care less if someone graduated eighth grade. True story. I could care less where they worked prior to me and I have the best team I've ever had in my life.

This is where the world is heading. And the truth is, it was uncovered by underdogs. It was uncovered by the people that couldn't afford it, or weren't smart enough, or had dyslexia, or tried a different path. I mean, George Washington, he had to change his whole life through self-education because by the time he was old enough to go to school, his family was broke. He didn't get to go to college. He had to study all on his own through self-education and look at the impact he made. But that's only one story of millions.

Looking back it was a blessing that I had no other options in my life and I had to reach out and try to learn from others who had already done what I was hoping to do. I had no option to go back to business school or try to get my master's degree. If desperation and being resourceful (two strong underdog advantages) didn't push me to find others I could learn from, Motor Millions would have been dead in the water. If I hadn't gotten involved in masterminds and group training, and gotten involved in workshops and learning from other people, I wouldn't have understood direct response marketing, and sales, and reciprocity, and building relationships, and then how to market on TV, and then eventually on YouTube and Instagram and Facebook. Most all of those strategies came from networking and through group- and self-education.

And here's the cool part, and I mentioned it earlier. This evolution has not only allowed you to have access to other people's knowledge, it also has opened up a window for you to make an impact on others and make a profit by sharing what you already know. By sharing a skill, a hobby, a passion, an expertise you have, even if you are just one year or one chapter ahead of other people you could help make self-education the new norm faster.

In fact, that's why Tony Robbins and I created the Knowledge Business Blueprint, the training and software to help the average person jump into the knowledge industry. And again, you can watch our two-hour training at kbbsecret.com.

Right now, let's get to your challenge. So what's one thing you learned from someone outside the traditional education system that moved the needle in your life the most?

How, today, can you change the framework or the way you look at things to go get more of that?

What course could you buy?

What mastermind could you enter?

What group training, what workshop could you attend?

What community could you belong to?

Who could you ask?

Who could be your mentor?

And then let's flip it on the other side:

Who could you mentor?

What superpowers do you have that would allow other people to go faster and quicker if they knew what you knew?

Are you a year, five years, ten years, twenty years ahead in a certain industry, where if you shared what you knew in a weekend, you could allow people to go five times faster?

Start thinking through that framework and then write an action step of what self-education you'll attend or share over the next ninety days.

Make this your new way of thinking and watch how complexity and stress start to melt and accomplishments start to pile up.

CHAPTER 6

Underdogs Don't Have to Care What Other People Think

I was in the special education reading class in my high school. Kids used to laugh at me when I read out loud. I don't think I bought a book to read for pleasure until I was in my early thirties.

And yet, as of today, I've written multiple *New York Times* best-selling books, and this is my sixth book.

How did I go from being a kid who literally graduated high school reading at an eighth-grade level, to being someone whose words are read by millions?

It doesn't make sense. In fact, I almost don't even believe it.

I'll tell you how it doesn't happen: you don't write books by listening to people who tell you the way it "has to be done."

But for a while, I did that.

You see, my first book was so bad that an editor told me I couldn't publish it. That it was so bad, she couldn't even edit it—like it was some other language or something!

I was literally one keystroke away from possibly never writing a book. I had the file up, and was about to delete it.

But I didn't. Something stopped me.

And that became one of the underdog advantages I've used to help me in all aspects of my career.

PRIVILEGED HAVE TO MAKE EVERYONE HAPPY

We all watch rich and famous people on TV and social media and think, "They have it made. They don't have to worry about what anyone thinks."

Let me tell you, that's about as wrong as it gets.

I have a lot of friends who are really famous, and pretty much all of them laugh when people say that. In fact, if there is anything they all uniformly hate about being famous, it's that most feel *they can't be themselves anymore.*

They have to answer to everyone: agents, managers, fans, paparazzi, haters, competitors—everyone.

The fact is, they have to worry what everyone else thinks, and they have to work to make them happy.

That's the thing about being in the spotlight: as soon as you are on stage, everything changes. Now everyone has an opinion, and now you have to pay attention to it.

I know, the same thing happened to me.

When I just had a collision repair shop and some real estate, I didn't have to really care much at all what anyone thought. I mean, I had some employees and some tenants, but for the most part, I was left alone.

But once I got my first infomercial up and running, man, the attention flooded in. Everyone wanted a piece of me. Yeah, this was really cool at first, after being ignored for so long.

But damn, pretty quickly, it got to be way more than I expected.

Because the thing that no one realizes when everyone wants a piece of you is that really everyone has expectations of you.

They expect you to be a certain way.

Or do things the way they want you to.

They're not afraid to tell you that you aren't being who they want you to be.

And it's not just expectations. The privileged have so many other disadvantages.

Everyone is always looking at them, expecting things. There are new pressures that you have to learn to grow into.

And when you are privileged, everyone wants to be around you, to be your friend. Everyone wants to jump aboard a train if it's heading to the promised land.

Most people never see this side of being privileged.

Now look, I'm not complaining and I bet no other successful person I know would take any of it back. Heck I would do it all over again 1,000 out of 1,000 times. And part of this new exposure is a damn good thing, of course. If they like you and your brand it helps your company, product, and life grow. In no way am I dismissing the valuable asset of exposure to fuel growth and brand recognition, it is definitely an advantage.

How's this a disadvantage? As you grow your brand or company, it seems to me there is a certain percentage of the world who are internally so envious of you moving forward, that they do things they hope will slow you down. Some misguided frustration about their own life, in my opinion. To them, your success leaves them feeling more stuck.

So they condemn you, criticize you, talk bad about you behind your back, and even go out of their way to sabotage you. The privileged have haters, and haters can do damage.

It's more than that though.

When you're privileged, you do get some advantages. Everyone is rooting for you, and the system works for you. You're in power, so other people in power help you.

Everything just goes your way...or so it seems to the underdogs on the outside.

But that's not how it actually works. In reality, the privileged have to follow the rules. They're always being watched, they have to answer to lots of other people. They have a target on their backs, and they can't make moves that people disagree with. The privileged have lots of stakeholders, and lots of public pressure, and people to answer to.

This means that the list of things that the privileged can use to help them starts to actually get smaller. They can't take wild risks. They can't do dangerous things. They can't do things that might make them look foolish—they have to get permission.

Because of this, the privileged can't take the risks they used to before the success came flooding in. When you have lots of people depending on you, when your every move is under the microscope, risks don't work.

This is why so many privileged fail once they get to the top. Harvard Business School professor Clayton Christensen became pretty famous for doing the research to prove that this is the case in business. He called it "The Innovator's Dilemma" and basically what he proved is that market-leading companies (the privileged) can do everything right, but still lose.

Here's how it works (and these lessons apply to several upcoming Underdog Advantages, not just this one):

1. Value is created most easily at the early and middle stages of any endeavor, so that by the time a company gets to be a big dog, it's much harder to make improvements.

2. Big companies have high expectations and very few ways to improve, but the underdogs have lots of room to grow and several smaller markets to focus on that the privileged can't.

OK, so what does this fancy business book have to do with you?

The point is simple: the privileged, just by virtue of their size and position, don't have the advantages that they once enjoyed...when they were underdogs.

This means that the privileged can't go after bigger issues. They are slow and bloated and have to worry about the underdogs being able to do the things they can't do.

Basically, they are stuck.

Now this sounds like I just shit on being successful. That once you get it, you will lose it. That is not the case at all. What you are learning in this book is to be or think like an underdog always, and you can grow year after year after year.

This mindset has allowed me and so many others to grow their success for decades. I mean I went from selling firewood, fixing cars, doing real estate, course creation, being an author, doing live events, and being a knowledge business leader, to typing these words of my sixth book. I may not always be perfect and I have surely failed miserably in between much of this. But as I wrote in my last book, *Millionaire Success Habits*, I adopted new habits in my life that helped make success sustainable.

But what I did not share in that book that I'm sharing here now is that I approached each of these endeavors as an outnumbered, under-resourced, under-funded, undereducated, underestimated underdog. I keep that underdog mindset alive and well, no matter what the numbers are, how privileged I've become, or who I partner with.

HOW I ALMOST DELETED A *NEW YORK TIMES* BEST SELLER

I wrote my first book because I realized the vast majority of my customers from my first self-education course refunded because of crap happening in their personal lives, limiting beliefs, and negative people in their lives, and it had nothing to do with what I created.

After I figured out Motor Millions and had it running successfully on TV, I was still pretty small-time and lean. I didn't have a lot of money, because it took so much investment to get it going, but it was going and I was making money.

But one thing was confusing the hell out of me: I couldn't understand why there was a 15 percent refund rate across the board.

The biggest money that went out every month was people refunding. This made no sense to me. I know I delivered. In fact, I over-delivered. I know for a fact that everything in Motor Millions worked, because I had personally made a lot of money doing it, and all kinds of other people—the ones who had actually done the work—were telling me the same thing.

I just didn't get it. I was beating myself up, asking, what is the problem? Like, what did I screw up? What could it be?

So I went and sat in on customer service for two weeks. I literally wore a headset and I listened to people calling in to complain. I spent like four hours every single day, listening to them.

And what I heard shocked me:

"I thought I'd have more time."

"My husband knows I got the course and doesn't support me."

"I don't think I'm smart enough to do this."

"I'm scared I'm going to screw it up."

"It won't work where I live."

I was expecting all the people to say things like, "The third module doesn't work!" but virtually none of the complaints were about the course itself. The majority were ALL about why they couldn't implement the course in their lives.

That's why I decided to write a book: to help clean out the

cluttered thinking in their heads, so they would be able to use my training.

There was a small problem: I'd probably read about five books in my entire life. In fact, I doubt if I had a book in my house or even owned a book at all.

I know, that's bad. I don't recommend that. Today, I probably burn through a book every ten days, but at the time, I was...less enthused about reading. It was before I discovered audiobooks.

But funny enough, I wasn't that worried about writing. Yeah, I knew that I'd need editing of course, but I also knew I had something to say and I knew I could help people get past these obstacles, so I just let it rip.

I have to be honest, since I had barely read any books in my life I wasn't sure where to start. I went to a book store, browsed top sellers, saw how they laid out chapters, went home, opened an ice-cold beer and spent the better part of a day just laying out what the hell I was going to write about.

It was truly painstaking at first, and then trying to figure out what went first only to realize the order was wrong ten different times. I knew what I wanted to say in my head but it just never came out exactly the same on paper. Well, at least when I first started.

After countless rewrites, overthinking, and months of tweaking, I ended up with a draft of something I thought had some solid potential. I mean, it was some of the same things Tony Robbins helped me with many years prior, along with so many things I'd learned along my personal success journey.

So I found a very well-regarded editor who lived in Virginia. Somebody told me she was the best editor there was, she'd edited a lot of *New York Times* best sellers, and had the reputation as the editor that tells you if it's right or wrong, and how to clean it up.

She wasn't cheap, but I spent the money to hire her. We had some great conversations back and forth. Then, instead of emailing the manuscript to her, I decided to deliver it in person. I was excited for god's sake. I flew from Phoenix all the way to some little town in Virginia where she lives.

When I got to her office, we sat down and I lit her up with my energy. Before I even handed her the manuscript, I told her all about myself and my passion. I told her why I wrote the book, and how this could help people. She got as fired up as I was:

"Oh my God, I'm so excited to work on this with you! I'll start editing it right now. Go back to your hotel, and let's meet here tomorrow to go over my first notes."

She called me the next morning at the hotel:

"Dean, you don't need to come over. This doesn't need an edit. It needs a complete rewrite. It's not a book. You can't even try to publish this. In fact, I can't even take your money."

After she was so excited, I was kinda flabbergasted. I asked why she thought this.

"Dean, it's a 220-page conversation. You can't write a book like you talk. Writers can break some rules, but you broke every rule. I'm sorry, it's just not a book."

I hung up.

I was so depressed. I had dumped my soul into that book. I really thought it was good. Yeah, of course the writing wasn't good, but the message...that was me.

And then I got down on myself, like I had done many times before whenever I came to a crossroads in my life. I allowed those inner limiting beliefs we all have (or at least an underdog like me had) to surface, and it wasn't pretty.

"What the hell is wrong with me? Why did I think I could write a book? I don't read books. I don't even own a book! I was in the special ed reading class in high school because my dyslexia was so bad I couldn't read out loud in class."

Basically, I remember literally saying to myself:

"Dean, you're a fucking idiot. Why would you think you could write a book? You're a collision repair guy who was lucky enough to create a working infomercial to sell your course, you're not an author. You're so stupid!"

I spun around like this for weeks, and I was feeling really bad about myself. The turning point came when I was literally an inch away from deleting the book. I remember it so clearly. I was on my black and very boxy IBM Thinkpad and saying to myself, fuck it. I thought:

"She didn't say it was just OK. She said, 'It's not a book, Dean. I'm sorry. It's not even editable. I spent two hours on the first page.' This is so bad. I just need to delete this and move on."

But I didn't. To this day, I can't honestly tell you precisely why I didn't delete it.

But when I think back, I believe that, deep down, I knew I had a good story, and I knew people needed what I wrote, and I knew it could work...if it could just be written a little better.

So I didn't delete it.

I saved it, just in case, one day, someone could make something of it.

UNDERDOGS DON'T HAVE TO CARE WHAT PEOPLE THINK

One of the best parts of being an underdog is the freedom that comes with it.

Yeah, it sucks to have no one watching you or paying attention, but when that happens, you have total and complete freedom to do anything you want. You can experiment. You can be goofy. You can dance like no one is watching—because they aren't.

What's crazy is that this is how most new and revolutionary ideas develop—far out of the mainstream.

The Wright Brothers developed the first plane on a sand dune in Kitty Hawk, North Carolina. That's as far out of the mainstream as you can get.

Apple and Google and Hewlett Packard were started in garages.

The examples go on and on and on. In fact, it's harder to find examples of big developments that do NOT happen outside of the mainstream.

This is because when you're an underdog, you don't have to worry about anyone else's opinion. You don't have to try and reach a consensus. You can just do your thing, experiment, have fun, and see what happens.

Quite frankly, being an underdog means you can grow and develop in peace, which is an incredible advantage.

This also gives you the gift of being underestimated. There is nothing better than low expectations. When people aren't expecting anything, they are far more likely to be surprised and impressed. You have the chance to really do something incredible.

Underdogs also have the space to work on themselves without being distracted.

You probably have no problem reading this book right now. But what if you had to read it out loud, in front of 1,000 people. I don't know about you, but I couldn't even read in front of my school class, much less in front of 1,000 people. Even the thought of it is nerve-wracking.

Don't get me wrong, I love what I do, but wow, if I mess up a speech in front of thousands of people, that is really bad. It's just more pressure.

This is why being an underdog is such an incredible advantage. You can work and test and develop in peace. If you fail, there is no one there to criticize you. If you have setbacks, it's no big deal, there's no pressure on you. You can just keep going, keep testing, keep trying, and work without the intense pressure of being in the spotlight.

Underdogs also get to see who their real friends are. When you're struggling and fighting to get ahead, no one cares about helping you. They all want to be friends with the privileged. We all know the saying, "The only time a bank wants to loan you money is when you don't need it."

Friendship works the same way.

That's why being an underdog is an advantage; you can meet and befriend the people who actually like you and care about you for you. You can make real and authentic friendships and relationships that last your whole life, because they're based on who you each are.

Why do you think so many celebrities and athletes have such a hard time finding true love?

Because how can they know if it's true, when the person met them because of who they are on the outside?

How can they really trust that this person cares about them as a person, and not them as a celebrity?

It's definitely harder.

But underdogs, they can. They can know who really loves them and who really cares for them, because they cared back when there was no other benefit to it.

We all know the saying, "Better to ask forgiveness than

permission." This is one of the best advantages of the underdog.

My favorite example of this from business is Ralph Lipshitz. Ralph was a Jewish immigrant to America, who grew up in a poor Bronx neighborhood. He grew up seeing the fabulous rich people in New York, with their iconic style, and wanted to bring that style to more people.

But that wasn't possible. Only big shots were in fashion. Who would ever want to wear something by Ralph Lipshitz? Though there were many Jewish people in the textile business, there were very few in high fashion. The high fashion industry at the time was totally controlled by older protestants; it was unheard of for a Jew to come into this world and sell to non-Jews (this was a long time ago, obviously).

But that's the thing; because Ralph was just one guy, no one really paid attention. Ralph didn't need to ask for permission. He just started selling ties and shirts with his iconic emblem on them. Within two years, Bloomingdales gave him an in-store boutique—the first time they'd ever done that.

He did make one concession to the world of the big dogs: he changed his name from Ralph Lipshitz to the name you probably know him by: Ralph Lauren.

This is what's so great about being an underdog—you don't have to worry about the rules. You don't have to care about "the way we do things." You can ignore all the norms that hold most people back. You can just go for it, because for the most part, no one is watching. No one cares what small-time underdogs do.

Yeah, if it works there will come a time that people will care—Ralph Lauren eventually had to deal with all the problems of being a big dog—but that's a great challenge to handle when that time comes.

And I don't know Ralph personally, but I would venture to say that he has carried his underdog advantages with him through his entire career, and that is why Ralph Lauren and Polo have stayed so relevant for so long.

The underdog can get out in front of them, take risks, and go for the big score—because there is almost no competition out there.

"IT WAS PUBLISHED? AND IT DID WHAT?"

About three months after I almost deleted my book I went back and started looking at it again. Now with nothing to lose, I looked at it through a different lens. Like, who the hell cares what she thinks?

And the truth is I loved it. More now than before. Yes, I realize I broke every rule of writing, but I accomplished exactly what it was I hoped to do.

I wanted to create a book to help people overcome their own limiting beliefs and turn them into empowering ones. I wanted to give everyday people like me a simple roadmap to stay the course, to take action, and not give up on finding a next-level version of themselves.

The book did all that. In fact, reading my own words empowered me even more, since ironically I was dealing with those same emotions I was teaching regarding my decision to publish or not to publish.

When done reading the book in a different light, I decided at that very moment that I truly had nothing to lose, that the editor was wrong, and that I was going to get this book published if it was the last thing I did.

So I found someone locally to edit the book and help clean it up. I remember saying to the editor:

"Just clean it up as best you can without changing my words and style, and try to make it so I don't look completely stupid." As you can tell I have a very vast and elegant vocabulary.

I carried that same confidence into a possible book publisher's office a few weeks later. Not sure if he loved the book or not, but I could tell he was impressed with my passion and I convinced him to take me on as a client.

Us underdogs surely find a way to be passionate about what we do, because we are so used to trying to convince others to believe in us when they have no reason to do so.

Within a month I had a book deal and about ten months later, my first book, *Totally Fulfilled*, became a *New York Times* best seller. For two weeks. Then it was off forever, but how many people can say that their very first book, that was almost deleted, made the highly prestigious *New York Times* Best Sellers list?

Though it wasn't a blockbuster seller, in the course of my life, this book was massive because it showed me the proof I needed to keep going, even when others said it wouldn't work. It gave me the courage to write my next book with more authority and confidence. My second book went on to sell a million copies. If I had deleted that first book, if I had listened to her, I'm not sure I'd ever have written a second book. Most likely, I would have been done.

I think about that a lot. I don't even blame that editor. Yeah, she was pretty awful crushing my dreams, but I don't think she was trying to hurt me. In fact, she taught me a great lesson:

I didn't have to listen to other people or worry what they think and neither do you.

Her telling me my book was terrible was actually really freeing, in a way. Once I got past the pain of it, it allowed me to totally let go of whether it was good or not, and just focus on doing what I could do best: help people. She freed me from any expectation.

I know there's a lot of people that don't feel like they could write a book. Or they wish they could do something else, but you don't because you don't feel qualified, or maybe you don't feel like the "right" people think highly of you or have your back. Well, what if they are all wrong? What if your inner doubt is flawed? What if you just changed that disadvantage to an advantage today? Remember, I wasn't qualified. Not at all.

But that doesn't matter. Being "qualified" just means you value others' opinions more than your own. That's a disadvantage.

But us underdogs, we can just focus on ourselves and what we are doing right—we don't have to worry about them.

And I have to admit it: when *Totally Fulfilled* hit the *New York Times* Best Sellers list, I took a picture of it...and mailed it to the editor who told me my book sucked.

I never heard back from her. I wonder why :)

UNDERDOG CHALLENGE #6

In this chapter, I decided to share the story of my first book being published. I've shared that story in public before, but never in this much detail, and I hope along the journey of the story you recognized something in yourself. Maybe you had a similar event, a similar issue, a similar person.

So many underdogs—like me—feel we need permission from someone, even though they might not be qualified to say, "Yes," or, "No." Because we don't have the resources, because we're not privileged, because we might not have the money or this expertise or the smarts or we're going into an area that's new, we feel like we need validation. We still want permission or we still care what other people think, and it took me a long time to get past this.

Does this sound familiar: you let your single friend give you advice on how to fix your relationship. You let your broke friend tell you how to start a business or make money. You let your miserable friend tell you how you should be happy.

I know I used to fall victim to that.

We somehow allow people in our lives to influence us, even if it's just cumulative, even if your negative friend tells you how to be positive, and you go, "Oh, she's always negative," but a piece of that lingers, and then you pull a little piece from the media, and you pull a little piece from your parents, and all of a sudden, it's enough to hold you back because you are looking for permission.

The reason I chose the *Totally Fulfilled* book story, even though I have 1,000 examples of people telling me I can't, or me wanting their permission and still going forward, I chose that because a book is so specific. A book seemed like such an impossible goal to me. I felt like someone had to be so smart and have proper grammar and proper English and follow every rule and have read one hundred books to be allowed to write one.

All of those things that I believed were bullshit, but then, even though I said, "Bullshit," and I wrote the book, when I finally hired an editor with great credentials, and she said, "No," I almost hit the delete button.

Where in your life are you about to hit the delete button on your metaphorical book that could have been a *New York Times* best seller?

It could be anything in your life, the new company, the new website you want to launch, the app you want to create, the invention you want to create.

What did you put on hold in your life because you didn't

get the permission, the validation, or the advice you were looking for when you wanted to go for it, and how can you set new parameters in place that don't allow bad advice to alter your bigger future?

CHAPTER 7

Underdogs Turn Desperation into Persuasion

When I was seventeen years old, my dad had a used car lot. If we're being honest, it wasn't much. At any given time there were six or eight cars, maybe twelve at most.

Since I was still in high school half of the day, most of the time my Dad would be the one to go out front when someone was looking at a car, to try and sell it to them. Except for Saturdays when I worked the whole day there. When we noticed a potential buyer scouting out the cars, I would joke with my dad and say, "Do you want to go outside and talk those people to death, or do you want me to go out there and actually sell them a car?" And he'd laugh and say, "You little bastard," with a big smile on his face.

178 · THE UNDERDOG ADVANTAGE

But the truth of the matter is I probably outsold my dad four to one.

How is that possible? How could a seventeen-year-old kid with minimal life experience, who had no sales training, and didn't know the mechanics of a close, outsell a grown man who'd been around and selling cars his whole adult life?

This is the most powerful, impact-making, profit-generating underdog advantage of them all. One I didn't fully recognize in myself until many years later. I had so much desperation to get out of what I was doing, to not be left behind, to prove everyone wrong, to become somebody, that I turned that desperation into an innate ability to persuade and sell effortlessly at a level most professional salespeople could never reach. And believe me I'm not alone. More on that soon.

First, back to my Dad. A big part of it was, or so I believe, deep down he didn't like selling. Maybe he felt it was demeaning in a way, he was self-conscious about it, and he felt like people should be able to figure out on their own that he had the best used cars around so they should just buy it or not. So he had this style that was a weird mix of both being very pushy, but also very hands-off. It didn't work well.

GO TAKE THE FREE, 30-DAY BETTER LIFE CHALLENGE AT THEBETTERLIFE.COM FOR TRANSFORMATION AND PRIZES.

I got good at sales because my desperation to achieve more transmuted into authenticity and enthusiasm and killer sales stats. What the heck does that mean? As an underdog, we have to persuade people to say yes. Yes to believing in us, yes to new partners, yes to getting people to take action on a damn dream, yes to loans, get a yes from your parents or significant other to have your back. We are always fighting for the yes because we are not privileged, and those underdogs that excel to the highest level master the art of persuasion without even trying.

I figured out something out that was so very simple, that I wondered why my dad and everyone else wasn't doing the same: you ready for this? I'd just listen to them. I'd ask them what they're looking for, and then listen more. When they were done, I'd ask another question and once again listen. I found out they would tell me everything and actually give me everything I needed to understand their fears, their wants, and their needs. I didn't think it was revolutionary, it just worked.

I listened so well and was so damn transparent with them that if what they wanted a sort of car that wasn't on our lot, I wouldn't try to sell anything to them. I was simply honest. Not that my dad wasn't, he just had a different approach.

But if we had a car that fit their profile, you can bet two

shiny nickels I got that sale with minimal words, effort, or pushiness.

And looking back, the confidence to make those sales happen without feeling bad or pushy like some people do, stemmed from one thing. The same thing goes today and why I have zero hesitation to push someone into a sale of one of my books, courses, or events.

Back then I knew something about my dad that no one else did: he made his used cars amazing.

Since he was a mechanic and repairman, before he put these cars on his lot, he did a ton of work on them. They would come to the lot in bad shape, but by the time he put them out to sell, they were fantastic.

For me, this changed everything. I knew these cars were killer, and I knew if the person I was talking to didn't buy that used car, they'd go buy someone else's potential lemon. If that car was the right match for them, then I felt like I had an obligation to get them to buy it so they would get the best value.

As I started getting into buying homes and converting them into apartments, I did the same thing. I'd renovate great apartments, better than what was out there in the nearby area, I'd love them so much that I'd feel like I was doing people a disservice if I didn't rent one of my apartments.

And I did that when I sold houses and sold courses on info-mercials. This has been my approach to everything I do in life.

Simply put, I make what I'm selling so good that I no longer feel like I'm "selling" it. I feel like I am persuading people to make their lives better.

WHY THIS IS THE KEY TO ALL UNDERDOG ADVANTAGES

I know this might sound unusual. Some of you might be resistant to selling. You may even doubt that selling is a good thing—or worse, you might think it's a bad thing.

But stop and think about that. Most likely you have this book in your hands right now because I persuaded you to buy through a sales video.

But aren't you glad I did? Seriously.

Maybe you doubted it at first, but now that you are here in the book and gaining underdog advantages from real-world experience, would you reverse that decision? Would you take twice the money back but the knowledge was erased from your brain if I offered it to you?

In my experience, because I've asked audiences of 7,000

people that same question and never had one hand go up, I can tell you the answer is no.

That is the main underdog advantage that I learned to harness, the difference between me and my father years ago, and between me and most people now:

Most people approach selling from a desperate position. They are desperate to sell, and they hate that feeling, so either they don't sell, or they sell in a way that pushes people away.

What we've seen with underdogs is that they can convert their desperation into action, which leads to authentic impact, which helps them persuade and sell in the best possible way. This is basically the magic formula for success.

I've seen so many underdogs that want it and are desperate, but they don't know how to convert it. They think if they build it, people will just come. They think if they just put their passion into it, make the product, the service, or the store amazing, that people will find them and business will flourish.

But that's not how it works.

Most people use very traditional sales and marketing strategies. They just talk about themselves and their product and they do the "debate team" type stuff. They aren't impacting from the heart.

Even the underdogs who use all the other advantages won't move past a certain level of impact, income, and wealth without this. In most cases that I have witnessed, without authentic and ethical skills to persuade people to action, your next level of life will elude you.

Underdogs that thrive do this.

In every super-successful underdog I have ever met, they become authentic, persuasive, in some cases the most amazing salespeople, negotiators, and deal-closers on the planet. And they do this because they truly believe what they are selling is helping people while simultaneously, the underdog desperation has never left them. Hopefully it never does for any of us.

Even if you intuitively feel as you read this, "Oh, that's not me. You had me with these other chapters about an underdog, but I don't like to do sales," I'm going to call bullshit.

The truth of the matter is nothing in the world happens without a sale.

I don't necessarily mean just money changing hands. Nothing in the world happens unless you make the sale. Yes, selling is persuading someone to take an action. it's that simple.

Whether that's starting a business, scaling the business you already own, making more impact, shifting careers, getting a raise in your current employment—all of it starts with persuasion followed by action (again, which is sales).

If you have a negative association to selling, that just means that at one point in your life somebody sold you something that you didn't want or maybe worse, someone took advantage of you.

I'm sorry if that happened, but I'm not sorry that we are about to change your entire outlook on selling and make you the best on the planet at it.

Could you actually be hurting people by NOT selling them?

I walked out on stage in front of over a thousand amazing business women, all entrepreneurs, wanting to go to the next level.

I started off, "Who here has their own company, or is starting one?"

Every single woman in the audience raised their hands.

And I said "OK, great, who'd like to go to another level, make more money? Have more freedom? Have more control?"

Everybody, once again, raised their hands. I said "Who's excited? Who's ready to live into their full potential?"

All of them start to cheer, now they were all excited.

Then I said "Now let me ask you this, if you're being honest, who in this room has a dislike, or even a slight apprehension, to selling?"

Ninety percent of the room raised their hand.

Very typical to the other tens of thousands of people I've asked that same question to on stage. The hard part of that is that I know that none of them will reach their desired goals without the underdog advantage of taking their passion, taking their desperation and turning it into effective persuasion.

I know like I'd done many times before, this killer group of ladies needed me to shift their perspective on selling.

So I get serious, "First off, the host introduced me by asking me for my ultimate selling secret. How did you do over a billion dollars in sales with your brands and your companies starting from nothing? How do you sell so well? How do you make it feel like it's not even selling? Just like all the way back in the car selling days with my dad. It's an easier answer than most people will expect to hear: love what you do, love what you sell, love your service, love your product, love your book, love your mastermind, so much that you know you're doing the world a disservice if you don't get them to give you a credit card. I want you to start looking through those eyes."

I said, "Do me a favor again and raise your hand if you were one of the ladies who was a little apprehensive about selling."

Once again 90 percent of the room raised their hands and I singled out this woman in the third row. I said "Tell me what it is that you do."

She said, "Well, I help moms, after they have a baby, get their identity back. I know when I had my baby, I felt so out of shape, I felt disconnected to my friends, my whole life was turned upside down, the attention wasn't on me anymore. Everything was about the baby, there was no sleep. I probably had postpartum depression, I felt horrible about it. It was so debilitating that I pulled myself up using a system I created, and I resurrected myself. So I decided to go into the business of helping other moms after they've had a baby, get back quicker, feel confident, feel sexy, and feel alive faster. To feel amazing about themselves."

I said "Wow, that's amazing. Tell me a story about a mom you've helped."

She perked up and her shoulders straightened up, her head lifted up, and her face lit up. And she told the most amazing story of this mom who was in a really bad place, and she helped get her back, better than ever, "Oh my god, I watched her go from on the verge of depression and feeling crazy to an abundance of happiness, looking and feeling sexy, with a huge joy for life again."

So I said, "Do you really love doing it?"

She says, "Oh my god, It's the greatest gift in the entire world."

And I paused and I said to her, "Well, do you suck at it?"

She went, "What? Wait! Um, NO! I'm amazing at it!"

And I said, "So you are just bullshiting me then, you're just pretending that you like to help people?"

She was like, "No!"

I could tell she was confused, maybe even getting a little upset, I could see her shoulders kind of slump, and she looked at me and said, "Why would you say that, this is my life now, it's my passion, it's my love."

I said "OK, but you also raised your hand that you don't like selling."

She was like, "True, I don't like selling."

I said, "So, I guess that means you don't actually care about helping people."

Once again she was confused, "What?"

I continued, "The women who need you, the women out there right now suffering, going through postpartum depression, who don't know what to do to fix it, who feel depressed in the middle of the night, but aren't telling anybody. They feel like they should be grateful for what they have, but they don't. They even feel weird holding their child. They don't feel sexy around their husband, they feel like they are going to get a divorce, they feel like they are going crazy, they feel like they should be happy. There are women going through that right now, that need you, but because you are afraid to promote, you're afraid to market, you're afraid to sell, they will never get your help. To hell with them right? You don't like to sell, so screw those moms that need you."

She said, "No, that's not what I want. I want to help."

I continued, "Well, only two things can happen if you don't persuade them or sell them to work with you. One, they go to someone else, who doesn't care at the level that you do. Who doesn't provide the services that you provide. Or they do nothing and they suffer, because you feel bad about selling. You have a moral obligation to sell, to promote, to let the world know of your amazing service, because those women need you."

You could have heard a pin drop in that room.

I waited a few seconds, and I said, "What do you think about selling now?"

And she said, "I'm going to be the best in the world at it."

I could feel how sincere she was, I remember getting literal goosebumps.

I thanked her and then turned my attention to the audience and said, "Now, who else in here has a completely different perspective on selling?"

The whole audience raised their hands.

Then I asked, "Who in here wants to learn to actually LOVE selling?"

Once again the entire room raised their hands.

This isn't just about business and starting or scaling your income. This is for everyone in all aspects of life who wants to make an impact or a difference in the world.

Let me ask you this, do you think Mother Theresa was a saleswoman?

Damn right she was, one of the best on the planet!

How many nuns do you think had the same exact heart

as Mother Theresa? A lot. I bet you countless numbers of them, and other Christians alike, had the same heart to provoke change and make a difference. So what separated her from them?

She was massively persuasive and I guarantee she used the underdog advantage of converting her desperation in the ability to sell people to take action, follow her, and align with her cause. It was common knowledge that when she had a vision or wanted something done, she sold other people in droves to jump in and support her.

Look at the impact she made on the world.

Do you think Martin Luther King, Jr. was a salesman?

No, of course not, he was a leader!

You sure the two things are different?

If Martin Luther King, Jr. just had that desire, that dream, to make a difference in the world but decided he would keep it to himself—what would have happened then? If he hadn't gotten onto thousands of church pulpits and in front of cameras and on stages—what happens then?

What if he just sat home and said, "Well, I have a huge dream but also a bit of apprehension to selling. Maybe if I just pray enough, if I just think it'll change, it'll just change on its own."

You're laughing right now because that's obviously absurd... yet I bet this is how you may approach sales and persuasion in your life.

We were subconsciously taught that if we just get better at what we do, if we become the best coach on the planet, or have the best product on the planet, or write the best book on the planet, people will come on their own.

That's a lie. They will never come.

Because you're missing the most fundamental thing. Selling is the oxygen, it is the breath of every single successful company in the world.

It's the foundation for success in all areas of life. And once you adopt a different way to look at it and do it with the best intentions, your life will never be the same.

I'll be totally honest: I'm trying to persuade you right now.

I'm trying to persuade you to see your life in a new way.

I'm trying to persuade you to see the things you thought held you back, can instead be what propels you forward.

I'm trying to persuade you to not just agree with what I'm

saying, I'm trying to get you to use this new perspective to compel you to act differently.

I'm trying to persuade you into real change in your life.

You can build the greatest product in the world, but if you don't market and sell it, no one is going to buy it. It's just the way it goes.

This may be the most important thing you need to learn right now and reiterating the fact that if you build it, no matter how good it is, no matter how strong it is, no matter how amazing it is, people will not come, unless you persuade them to take action.

All of the other things in this book are amazing, but if you're going to start or scale your own company, if you want to start masterminds or training courses, or help other people go faster, if you want to be a coach—none of this will happen unless you sell.

The three things that are so important in persuasion are these: Love what you do so much you feel that you're doing people a disservice if you don't get them to take action. That's step one.

Two, live authentically, be the best version of you. Don't try to be another salesperson, don't be a version of you that you saw in someone else, just be the real you. Speak through your heart and share even the most painful moments in your life, if that allows people to see the real you.

Third, step into persuasion with confidence. So many people, when it's time to sell—I watched my dad do it, I watch people do it on stage, I watch people do it when I'm face to face with them—they'll talk about their product, like this woman did when she was talking about helping moms, but when it gets to the sales part, people get embarrassed or lose their confidence and the sale simply never happens.

If you love what you do, amp up your confidence, step into the sales process, step into the persuasion. You are helping people go to another level. When you do that with quiet confidence, with humble power, with authenticity, with passion, people notice. Being real and raw...If you're in sales, your sales will double. If you're not in sales, or your business isn't at the level that you want, you'll watch your income grow.

Nothing happens without persuasion followed by action (selling). Selling is not evil; it's the launching pad to next-level impact and income.

Fix it until you love it, and then go out there and sell it with all your heart.

UNDERDOG CHALLENGE #7

So, here's your challenge: Pick one of your favorite movies, one of your favorite books, or one of your favorite restaurants (it can be anything that you love, really).

I want you to persuade someone to use that thing you love. To eat at the restaurant, or watch that movie, or buy that book.

Start by thinking about what about this movie, this book, this restaurant, made you happy, what fulfilled you while you were reading, what made you cry and laugh while you were watching it, what made your stomach feel amazing while you were eating. Whatever it is, it enhanced your life. And as you tell your friend or relative about this book and you persuade them, I want you to think of what we talked about in here.

I want you to approach this thinking that if you don't get them to read the book, watch the movie or eat the food, you're doing them a disservice.

Then I want you to think about your physiology, meaning, how your body feels. When you like something, are your shoulders down or are your shoulders back? Do you have a frown or a smile? Of course you have a smile and your shoulders are back, you're standing tall. So think about that.

Secondly, when you like something, do you talk about it in

a low, monotone voice, or do you talk about it enthusiastically? As you share this movie, this book, this food, talk about it enthusiastically. Not arrogantly or annoying, but in an excited way.

Then, think of something personal in your life that connects you to what you are recommending. I love this Italian restaurant because it reminds me of my grandmother, just home-style cooking. I love this movie because it reminded me of a time when I was a kid and I felt desperation, and this movie brought me out of that. I love this book because the journey the author took you through made me realize that I can decide to become the best version of myself without anyone's permission.

Share something personal. While your shoulders are back, while you're smiling, while you're enthusiastic, be authentic at the deepest level possible on why you truly liked it. Find it in your soul, find it in your heart.

To recap: Pick something you love. Know you are doing them a disservice if they don't do what you ask. Be authentic and enthusiastic, and then simply step in to push for them to take the action with no apologies. Then watch what happens.

Your results will be unlike anything you have experienced and you will feel great about it.

Then I want you to pick something else. I want you to pick that business idea that you've been keeping inside, or the one that you've told a few people about but you did it in an embarrassed way or you hesitated, or you thought people would think you were crazy for wanting to do it and you didn't get a good reaction because you didn't present it the right way. You presented it almost apologizing. You presented without passion, without enthusiasm, without authenticity, without confidence.

I want you to revisit the business you want to do, the company you want to grow, the people you want to hire. Use these same principles to sell the people you work with, to sell your spouse, to get your kids to take an action that you want. Practice this underdog advantage this entire week and watch how your perspective on selling will grow and watch the yeses come flying in.

Conclusion

As we get to the end of this book, I want to make sure you understood my method on how I put this book together. In all transparency, I wanted to create a contrast between underdogs and the privileged.

But the truth is, I wasn't doing it to knock someone who is so-called "privileged." I just wanted to share that the underdog mentality is what drives success.

Listen, my kids are privileged. I can't replicate the fact that I grew up in a tiny little town, that I lived in a trailer park, that I had no money, that I wore hand-me-downs, that my parents' cars were so crappy that I made them drop me off two blocks from school, that I got made fun of so much.

I can't replicate that in my kids, but what I fight to do every day is to insert in their minds the underdog mindset, to be persuasive, to be resourceful, to not care what other people think, to not follow the norm, to not make decisions by committee, and all the other underdog advantages.

You see, at a young age, I admired people that came from

a so-called privileged background yet were still hungry. I remember—and this may have been before some of your time—John F. Kennedy, Jr. The guy was born with every privilege that exists on the planet. Six-foot something, tall, dark, handsome guy, great physique, well-spoken. He was a Kennedy for God's sake, pretty much American royalty. He was one of the wealthiest people alive, set to inherit the Kennedy fortune along with his sister, yet I admired him and so did the rest of the world for his hunger, for his fight, for his underdog mindset.

How do we explain that drive?

What most people didn't see was this underdog mindset. He fought in business, he fought to graduate top in his school. He started his own magazine called *George* and though it wasn't thriving out of the gate, he was hungry and fighting for it to grow. His untimely death obviously put an end to it, but I have zero doubts his underdog mindset would have made that a household name for life.

And I've obsessed on that. I've obsessed on it because I don't want my kids to be privileged and have a privileged mindset. So please know, throughout this entire book, I wasn't knocking the privileged.

I wanted to give you a contrast. I wanted to show one against the other.

So I don't care if you were born with millions of dollars in the bank. I don't care if you have the perfect job. I don't care if you're the CEO of a company or you're flat on your ass, broker than broke, desperate, and don't know what the hell to do with your life. It doesn't matter where you came from—it matters how you think.

Adopt these simple underdog advantages because they will give you superpowers that most people will never see coming.

I encourage you to unlock your underdog advantages, unleash your superpowers. Do not settle for what the world tells you that you deserve. Do not settle for what your teachers, or boss, coworkers, friends, and even family told you that you could have.

Before we end this book, there's a couple more quick things I'd like to share with you. So this isn't just a short read that gets you to think, but an actual guide to action. As I'm finishing the conclusion to this book, I just got back from a week's vacation in my hometown of Marlboro, New York, a town of 6,000 people, the town where I lived in a bathroom with my dad, where I struggled, and where I also became a millionaire.

About five years ago I bought my grandmother's old home, the place where I spent much of my childhood. It went up for sale, a friend called me to let me know, and I bought it immediately. The cool part about that house is my great-grandparents lived there, my grandparents, my mom, and now I get to spend time there with my kids. Heck, it was built in 1760.

It's a humble little place. As I walked around the property and through the little town, I ran into old friends, I drove past homes I used to live in, even the trailer park where we got evicted with my mom, who was trying to support us working two jobs to make $90 a week. It was pretty emotional for me.

I even hung out with some amazing old friends who I love dearly. They are still there with the same worries and the same stresses. It made me realize something: your past, your circumstances, the amount of resources you have— none of that dictates the future.

As we spent an entire chapter on, your resourcefulness does.

I was told by everybody in that little town as I grew up with big dreams, that success was for other people. It was for wealthy people, it was for people with the right colleges, it was for people with the right family who supported them. It was people who lived in New York City.

But they were all wrong.

And sometimes, all those outside voices stick and they

become inside voices. That inner self-doubt telling you that you don't have what it takes, that you don't have the privileges, that you don't have the advantages, is full of shit. And so are the people around you.

Is it easy? Hell no.

And at every level, you have to pull your underdog advantages out of yourself. Listen, you might not have the circumstances I had, or maybe they were way worse, doesn't matter.

I can remember clearly not only being broke in that little town, but also how I felt when I transcended that and actually became a millionaire in that same small town in my mid-twenties. By twenty-six I had a collision shop that was thriving, I had an auto sales business, I had thirty-something apartments, I was buying land and subdividing it and building houses.

But guess what? I knew there was more for me. I knew that I had more to give the world and I wasn't willing to settle. By everybody else's standards I had made it.

I was a broke kid who came from nothing and I was making more than both my parents combined. I was supporting my parents. I had new cars. I built the biggest house that little town had ever seen. I was living what seemed like an abundant life.

Yet, deep down, I was sad, feeling that I was the big fish in a little pond. I said to myself, "I don't give a fuck that I'm making 250 grand a year, that I'm a so-called big shot in a little town. I have more to give the world. I want to make more impact. I want to go to another level. No, I don't have the college education. No, I don't have the resources but I'm going to do it."

To do that, I had to tap into everything I shared with you in this book.

I had to alienate some friends.

I had family members stop talking to me.

I had to re-energize every underdog advantage and fight like I had zero privileges.

And you may go through the same sort of situation or feelings. From the outside, others would have thought I was privileged, lucky, or maybe that I should have just been happy considering where I came from. I was making more than 99 percent of the people in that little town, but to hell with that, I don't want to be a large bass in a little farm pond. I want to be a fucking whale in the ocean.

And I went for it and I risked everything. And I kept the

hunger and mindset of being an underdog even when on the outside I looked privileged.

So let me ask you, where are you in your life right now as you listen to or read this book?

Are you feeling that you have nothing going on for you and no advantages and no one's helped you?

Maybe it's a little different now that you're at the end of this book.

Maybe you're doing OK, but you feel like I felt when I was making 250 thousand dollars a year.

Maybe money's not an issue, but you want to make more of an impact on the world.

If you have to, go back and read this book again. Dig deep inside of you. Be resourceful. Find your groove, find your niche. Fight for it with your life because this is your life. We have one shot at it.

We weren't put on this earth for mediocrity, we weren't put on this earth to have a "good" life. We were put here to squeeze every bit of juice out of this life that God, the universe, gave us, to know that we didn't waste it, that we didn't throw it away, we didn't do what everybody else thought was cool.

What if you clear all the bullshit of what the world has shown you about what success means, or what it looks like on Instagram, or what your relatives perceive success is, and you figure out exactly what it means to YOU.

What fills your soul?

It doesn't mean you can do it today—but you can start today. Start the initiative now. The next five years are going to go by no matter what you do. And five years from now, you might be reading another book like this thinking, maybe it's time to get started. The time to get started is this very moment in life, now.

This is your call to action. I wrote this book to be short and powerful and to the point because I wanted to disturb you. I wanted to disturb you into an action. I want you to stop feeling sorry for the things that life didn't give you, and start looking in your tool chest again for the fucking ax and pick that's sharp as hell that's in there already, that you've been ignoring.

Your greatest disadvantage that you've been holding to your whole life may just be exactly what God or the universe gave you to be your own superhero, to tap into your full potential, to make more money, to create real wealth, to bring abundance and happiness and joy in your life, to have the freedom to know that you're living life on purpose.

So at the end, when we look back, we can say, "I did it."

Stop looking for the outside world to give you a hand, to open up the door. They're going to slam the door in your face over and over. Use these underdog advantages to break through that door.

And as we come to an end here, I want to give you an action step so this isn't just a quick read:

What are you going to do today, right now, this very moment to start the journey toward YOU 2.0? What can you do in the next sixty minutes to tap into the tool chest of your underdog advantages?

How can you turn those disadvantages into your rocket fuel?

What are you going to do to make more money, to have more freedom, to take control of your time?

Literally, stop listening, stop reading, and write down, what action you can take right now to start the momentum.

Are you going to register the URL?

Are you going to go watch the training with Tony Robbins and me and see how to tap into the knowledge industry?

Are you going to go after your dream?

Are you going to stop listening to negative people?

Are you going to stop listening to your parents, your husband, your wife—not that you have to love them less, but when are you going to stop letting the news and other people influence you?

What could you do right this minute?

In fact, let's get granular. What's one of the goals you now have?

What are you going to do in the next twenty-four hours to start the momentum for that same goal?

Then, what are you going to do in the next three days?

And the next seven days.

And the next month.

And the next three months.

And then the next six months.

Six months from the day you finish the book, what will that end goal look like?

And not just writing down what it looks like, I want you to project that we're already there, that you and I are having lunch six months from now and you're looking in my eyes and you say, "This is what I thought was a disadvantage, I turned it into an advantage and this is what I accomplished."

By six months from now you could have massive momentum. You could not only have reached your goal, but have a completely different mindset and be happy that you're an underdog.

I'd love to see your evolution and have you inspire others as well. Tag #underdog with your journey, with pictures of you with this book, or pictures of what you once thought was a disadvantage, share your breakthroughs. Let's help all the underdogs of the world unite and accomplish what they were designed to achieve.

I believe most of the world has a superhero locked inside and unfortunately, most everybody dies with it in there.

Using the underdog advantages is the key to letting your superhero out.

I can't wait to see what you do next.

RESORCES

Get More Ongoing And Personal Support
On Your Journey To You 2.0

Follow Me On Instagram For Daily Inspiration,
Teaching And Support!
@DeanGraziosi

Check Out The Millionaire Success Habits Podcast At...
Deanspodcast.com

See Why Our Youtube Channel Is One Of The Best Around...
www.youtube.com/Deangraziosi

**Want To Learn From Tony Robbins & I
On How To Impact People's Lives And
Get Paid For What You Already Know?**
Go Register For Our Special 2 Hour
Online Webcast For Free At...
KBBSECRET.COM

TAKE THE FREE "BETTER LIFE"
CHALLENGE

- ▶ Get A New 3 Minute Challenge Every Day For 30 Days!

- ▶ See How Small Shifts Can Create Huge Success In Your Life

- ▶ Earn Points For Completing Each Task And Earn Bonus Points For Sharing With Friends And Family

- ▶ Win Killer Prizes Each Month Like Ipads, Headphones, Apple Watches And MORE

- ▶ Earn A Shot At Winning A Brand New Car Absolutely Free!

www.TheBetterLife.com

See How A Few Minutes A Day Could Change Your Life Forever! **Plus You Have The Chance To Win a Brand New Car!**